CRAZY HORSE
WEEPS

THE CHALLENGE OF BEING LAKOTA
IN WHITE AMERICA

Joseph M. Marshall III

Author of *The Lakota Way* and
Hundred in the Hand

CRAZY HORSE
WEEPS

THE CHALLENGE OF BEING LAKOTA
IN WHITE AMERICA

FULCRUM

Library of Congress Cataloging-in-Publication Data

Names: Marshall, Joseph, 1945- author.
Title: Crazy Horse weeps : the challenge of being Lakota in white America / by Joseph M. Marshall III.
Description: Golden, CO : Fulcrum Publishing, [2019]
Identifiers: LCCN 2018061344 | ISBN 9781682750254
Subjects: LCSH: Lakota Indians--Ethnic identity. | Lakota Indians--History. | LCGFT: Essays.
Classification: LCC E99.T34 M358 2019 | DDC 978.004/975244--dc23
LC record available at https://lccn.loc.gov/2018061344

Printed in the United States of America.
0 9 8 7 6 5 4 3 2 1

Cover art by Jim Yellowhawk

Fulcrum Publishing
4690 Table Mountain Drive, Suite 100
Golden, Colorado 80403
800-992-2908 • 303-277-1623
fulcrumbookstore.ipgbook.com

Contents

Essays

Preface

One of the most heartbreaking stories I ever heard about Crazy Horse had nothing to do with battles or warfare. I could feel the tears welling up in my eyes when I heard how he wept at the burial scaffold of his daughter who had died of cholera. It became more meaningful, and more heartbreaking when I became a parent.

His heart was broken by the very tragedy that most of us fear more than death—the loss of a child. Though it is a lonely experience to the parents who have suffered this tragedy, the loss he and his wife endured was obviously not the first for Native parents at that point in our history. And it would not be the last. Furthermore, there is an added factor that even astute historians tend to overlook.

For Crazy Horse and his wife, Black Shawl, there was one unfortunate commonality with other Native parents who lost children in that era. The suffering and deaths of their beloved children (and many adults as well) was directly attributable to invading nonindigenous newcomers. I am, of course, referring to white people, the Europeans and then the Euro-Americans. The daughter of Crazy Horse and Black Shawl was afflicted with cholera, a disease unknown to the indigenous people of North America until the arrival of Europeans, and one for which the prior inhabitants of this continent had no immunity. Other diseases for which Native people had no immunity were measles, chicken pox, and smallpox. The latter, of course, was the most devastating for our ancestors.

In the broader context, had white people not come to North America, Crazy Horse and Black Shawl's daughter, whom they had named They Are Afraid of Her, would not have contracted cholera and would likely have lived a long life. But the horrific reality is that the Europeans did come and the Euro-Americans continued the invasion. The stage was set for Crazy Horse's daughter hundreds of years before she was born. If the Lakota had avoided contact with the invaders, perhaps the impact of diseases would have been less. But diseases were not the only consequence.

Difficult, sudden, unexpected, and even tragic change had fallen upon Crazy Horse's people long before the death of his daughter. Furthermore, this had been occurring for the indigenous people of Turtle Island (more or less the common pre-European name for North America among many indigenous nations) for at least three hundred years by then, attributable to the newcomers from Europe. It is difficult, perhaps impossible, to point to a particular moment and determine that as the point in time when change began to manifest negatively for indigenous people as a consequence of the newcomers' arrival.

Negative changes included displacement from villages, homelands, and hunting lands; confusing and convoluted interactions with the newcomers; untold numbers of deaths from unknown diseases; confrontations; battles; massacres; and in the end, long, drawn-out wars; broken promises; loss of lands; limited existence on reservations; and loss of culture. Of course, these rather antiseptic descriptions cannot fully describe the number and horrific nature of atrocities suffered by indigenous people at the hands of white people. There are too many, but a very short list includes the New England smallpox blankets, Trail of Tears, the Long Walk suffered by the Navajo, Sand Creek, and Wounded Knee.

A realistic description of each would be nearly impossible for most people to read. One example is the Sand Creek Massacre. It occurred in November of 1864, in which the 3rd Colo-

rado Volunteers under the command of Colonel John Chiving-
ton (a Methodist minister) attacked a Cheyenne and Arapaho
village encamped under a white flag at Sand Creek in eastern
Colorado. Days later the attackers paraded through the streets
of Denver with body parts of women and children attached to
their uniforms. Of course, one can only imagine how those body
parts became body parts. Multiply this kind of gut-wrenching
ugly reality by a few hundred, and perhaps the average non-Native American can dare to try to understand the real history of
North America in the past five hundred years.

Only now are white people, albeit still not enough, beginning to accept the extent to which their "conquest" of North
America decimated the indigenous peoples who had already been
here for tens of thousands of years. Regrettably and tragically,
there is not a point at which it stopped completely. Granted,
the physical atrocities have been fewer, but they are still occurring. And we must say that because of Wounded Knee in 1973,
and because the killing of Native peoples by police continues to
occur at the highest rate for any ethnic group, and because of
the use of military tactics and equipment by police against the
peaceful protests that began in 2016 against the oil pipeline in
North Dakota. But the frightening reality is that the attitudes
that enabled Manifest Destiny are still alive and are the basis for
racism and government policies and actions.

Those attitudes fostered the US government's policies and
actions that can be summed up in the phrase, "Kill the Indian
and save the man," the banner under which the assimilation
of Native peoples into American mainstream society occurred.
The consequences of those attitudes and policies have been the
continued diminishing of Native languages and culture, which
bears a further consequence that most of us Native peoples do
not see or want to see—the assimilation into white mainstream
culture. Furthermore, there is a darker and even more damag-

ing consequence—a skewed awareness of our own history, influenced heavily by white perspective.

We Lakota, and all indigenous descendants of the original Turtle Islanders, have endured much, to say the least, as previous paragraphs testify. We have lost much as well—initially homelands and territories, freedom, and ancient lifestyles. Yet we are on the cusp of losing more. Indeed we stand on the edge of losing it all. The fact of the matter is our final stronghold is not territory or a piece of land. Our final stronghold is our sense of identity.

Identity is simply defined as *the fact of being who or what a person or thing is.*

Our Lakota identity was strong and powerful. For countless generations we were hunter-gatherers and evolved into a cohesive and well-defined society with strong and necessary roles for males and females, a society that formed beliefs, customs, traditions, spirituality, and values based on the realities of a relationship with the natural environment. We understood our roles and our place within the reality of the natural order. We looked on the land as a relative and not a commodity. In short, we knew who we were and where we had come from. However, that began to change the moment the newcomers from Europe gained a foothold into our territories and a semblance of credence in our thinking.

Our Lakota identity is obviously not what it once was. It has been altered by two broad and insidious factors: intermarriage with Europeans and Euro-Americans and forced assimilation into the mainstream American culture. Intermarriage thinned our bloodlines and was a factor in the alarming swiftness by which assimilation was able to diminish our sense of who we were, and who we are.

A necessary, if not frightening question that each of us contemporary Lakota must ask ourselves is a simple one, though

I fear that while the answer may be simply given, the consequences of it are anything but simple: What language do we speak predominantly?

Even for first language Lakota speakers, the unscientific but honest answer is English.

I am a first language Lakota speaker, having learned it growing up with my maternal grandparents; Lakota was the language we spoke 99 percent of the time in our home. The other 1 percent was obviously English, and it occurred each day at six p.m. for fifteen minutes when our battery-powered radio was tuned to a radio station for news, and when my uncle came home from school and spoke English to me. I spoke, thought, and dreamed in Lakota. Only when I went away to school in 1953 at the age of eight did English become a consistent part of my life. And even then, all of the other students at the Kyle Bureau of Indian Affairs Day School on the Pine Ridge Reservation were bilingual. So while English was the language of the classroom, the conversations with my two closest friends at the school were in Lakota. Indeed, many playground conversations among the Lakota students, and any well away from the earshot of teachers and other white folks, were in Lakota. Even in the home of my paternal grandparents, with whom I was then living, Lakota was the predominant language, though both my grandparents and all of my aunts spoke English.

Beyond language, my maternal grandparents consistently reminded me who and what I was. *Nilakota*, they would say, which is "You are Lakota." This continued even after my two years at Kyle Day School, when I was returned to them. Furthermore, they reinforced that statement with stories told in Lakota. But the most impactful lessons and consistent reinforcement of our Lakota identity were in the way they lived their lives. To put it precisely, they did what they said. All of that resulted in my certainty about who and what I was. That certainty remains today.

The reality of these times, this era, is that even as a first language Lakota speaker, the language that I speak most of the time is English, and this book is obviously written in English. I still do think consistently in Lakota, however. The only person I always speak Lakota to and with is my mother, who is now ninety. As heartwarming as that may be, it represents a sad truth: first language speakers are getting older. A 2014 survey indicated the average age for a first-language Lakota speaker is seventy. This points to a harsh possibility—one that I hope never turns into a reality—that there will be a day, frighteningly sooner than we realize perhaps, when there will be no more first language Lakota speakers. We hope that would not mean the end of the Lakota language, but it certainly might mean that it would be affected by the lack of user patterns only first language speakers possess. And, as with the loss of any piece or aspect of culture that we have experienced over the past five or six generations, we would be losing yet another piece of our identity.

The second question we contemporary Lakota need to ask ourselves is: Do we live our lives *culturally* more as Lakota people or more in the mold of the society that forced assimilation upon us?

The number of households on Lakota reservations where the Lakota language is spoken predominantly is far from the majority. Akin to that is the reality that outwardly, and necessarily, our lifestyle is more mainstream America than it is Lakota. We live in small towns and communities on reservations and in larger towns and cities in the region and across this country; our children and grandchildren attend public schools, but even "Indian-controlled" schools are structured and operated by state codes and standards; we put our money in banks; buy power from utility companies; live in square houses with physical addresses; shop at grocery stores and indoor malls; worry about interest rates and politics; have an avid interest in our favorite sports teams; and some of us worship as Christians infrequently or regularly. And, perhaps most telling, most of us think in English.

The assumption made by some white Americans that a Native person is somehow a living, breathing repository of his or her particular tribe's culture, history, and language is simply wrong. Hence it is safe to assume that while there are approximately an estimated 170,000 Lakota people today, we are not all *culturally* Lakota. Far fewer than 30 percent of us speak our language, and 60 percent of us live off-reservation. While a number of us do practice and live our spiritual beliefs and observe pre-reservation customs and traditions, we are not in the majority, and perhaps not even in the plurality. And then there is that segment of our population, usually on or near the reservations, that is biologically Lakota but culturally white, and which often denies their Lakota heritage until they can gain some advantage from it—usually financial.

Why, then, are all of the aforementioned contemporary Lakota realities? The answer is simple, and soul shattering for some of us. Assimilation has worked and is working, and that leads us to the even more tragic reality that we are on the brink of losing our identity.

Crazy Horse knew that whites brought the sickness that took his daughter. To what extent that deepened his grief is impossible to know, if it did at all. Suffice to say he wept at her burial scaffold alone for days. He had been born into a time, about 1840, when whites were already steadily nibbling at the edges of Lakota territory and Lakota life. He grew up witnessing the unwanted and negative impacts on Lakota people and lifestyle that came with those newcomers. At the age of fifteen he saw firsthand the aftermath of General William Harney's attack on a Sicangu Lakota village on the Blue Water Creek, in what is now west-central Nebraska. An attack carried out while the village's leaders where in a parley with Harney himself. An aftermath that included a burned-out village and eviscerated corpses of women and children.

Beyond his personal losses, however, Crazy Horse knew full well that circumstances had changed unimaginably and likely irreparably for the Lakota because of the coming of the whites. He also knew that those unwanted changes would go beyond the loss of land and the great herds of bison. He was afraid that unwanted change would strike at the very core of being Lakota.

Perhaps, then, while he wept for his daughter, he was also weeping for the future generations of Lakota children who would see and feel the loss of who and what they were—their identity.

Yet, there is another reality, summed up in the innocuous axiom: if you do not know what you have, or had, you will not know what you have lost.

We Lakota today are not what our ancestors were. On the whole we do not live and breathe being Lakota the way they did. For us the sun does not rise on lands we controlled stretching away to the horizons, and we do not feel the thunder of the hooves of millions of bison. Our lands today are scarred by fences, roads, and soiled by toxic pollution, and our lives poisoned by racism and an uncertain future for our culture.

However, within us is the power and ability to rebuild and strengthen our culture, and perhaps with something as simple and effective as language immersion experiences for children, as well as adults, and perhaps something as simple as Lakota adults teaching Lakota history to Lakota children. Because it is in our children and grandchildren where the best hope rests for the future of our culture, and our identity as Lakota people.

By all accounts Crazy Horse was a doting father and loved his daughter dearly. As a matter of fact, he was sensitive to the needs of everyone in his village. It was a sensitivity born of genuine caring and compassion and went beyond his responsibilities as a leader. One wonders what he would think if he were to suddenly come back to this time and see the circumstances Lakota children are facing today.

Crazy Horse was born into a time that already knew the presence of white people. As a teenager he was an eyewitness to an unprovoked attack (the infamous Mormon cow incident*) on a Sicangu Lakota village by soldiers from nearby Fort Laramie in Wyoming Territory. The Lakota immediately counterattacked and routed the soldiers, killing nearly all of them. About a year later, he saw the aftermath of the US Army's retaliation for that attack, carried out against the Sicangu village on the Blue Water Creek, this time in what is now western Nebraska. In that attack, unspeakable atrocities were committed against Sicangu women and children by General William Harney's soldiers. Because of the ugliness he saw as a boy, Crazy Horse spent the rest of his life resisting the encroachment of whites to the point of facing them on the field of battle when it was necessary.

Another event that was likely the first portent of things yet to come occurred in the late spring before the Battle of the Greasy Grass. It began with Sitting Bull, the Hunkpapa medicine man and civilian leader, sending out a call for a gathering of the Lakota people to discuss ways to stem the tide of white encroachment. He had sent out messengers during the winter and then led his own people into the country south of the Elk, or Yellowstone River the following spring. Crazy Horse

---

*In September of 1854 a cow, belonging to a Mormon immigrant traveling the Oregon Trail near Fort Laramie in Wyoming Territory, wandered into a nearby Sicangu Lakota village, and was shot, butchered, and distributed for food. The owner demanded his cow be returned, and although the village headman offered mules in payment, the owner wanted the cow. A detachment of soldiers led by an Indian-hating officer went to the village to arrest the man who killed the cow. The village headman refused, the soldiers opened fire, and Lakota warriors responded, killing all but one soldier.

led his people to join Sitting Bull, and other Lakota broke away from the agency at Camp Robinson (in what is now northwest Nebraska) to join them. After a few weeks the combined group of Sitting Bull, Crazy Horse, and the breakaways numbered a few thousand. And the numbers would continue to grow as the weeks went by.

The gathering continued to move west and would, of course, eventually arrive at the valley of the Greasy Grass, or Little Bighorn River as the summer started in late June. Before the final move to Greasy Grass, Sitting Bull conducted a Sun Dance. He was, at the time and had been for many years, the most influential spiritual leader among the Lakota, and his decision to do the Sun Dance was to unify the people and bring about solidarity. During his preparation for the ceremony, he fasted and fell into a trance and was given a vision. It was that vision that likely became a strong impetus for the outcome of the battle that was to occur roughly a month later.

Sitting Bull's vision was graphic and carried an important message, a warning. He saw Long Knives (soldiers) and their horses, bloodied and falling from the sky into the midst of a Lakota village. The image, of course, foretold a victory, which kindled hope for a people tired of white encroachment—perhaps to the point that the vision's warning was overlooked, even ignored.

During the vision a voice told Sitting Bull, "I give you these because they have no ears," in reference to the Long Knives. The voice also warned *not to take anything that belonged to them,* the Long Knives. During the unfettered chaos of the Battle of the Greasy Grass, Lakota and Northern Cheyenne fighting men picked up firearms and ammunition from fallen soldiers, in what some Lakota later considered to be in contradiction to the warning.

There is, however, a broader context possible. The warning may not have been only about the soldiers' weapons, or it may not have been about the weapons at all. Perhaps the warning was about something more sinister. The words in the warning were *takun tawapi hena ayustanpo* or *takun tawapi hena ecupi snipo.* Translations are generally "leave what is theirs," or "do no take what is theirs."

The warning may not have been about *guns*, or *bullets*, or *things.* The warning might well have been about something that was far more devastating than guns or bullets. It might have been warning us *not to be like white people, not to take on their ways and their way of thinking.*

Retrospect is a powerful teacher, yet we Lakota have not followed that warning. We have not turned away from the "things" of the Long Knives, hence the "things" of the nation they represented, the nation that sent them to capture, subjugate, control, and kill our ancestors. In retrospect, we Lakota, if we are to be coldly honest about our history from 1876 to the present, have taken on the ways and thinking of the whites. Retrospect is a powerful teacher—if we heed the lessons.

It is entirely possible that the foregoing is the opinion of just one person—me. But it is also entirely possible that the assimilative process has effectively done the job it was designed to do. Therefore, we are allowing our language to die, allowing skewed versions of our history to be taught in schools, and allowing Christianity to continue its onslaught on our spiritual beliefs.

If we truly care about our culture, and whether it will exist in the future, we need to think what we ourselves have done to further assimilation. We need to stop accommodating the colonizers by allowing them to appropriate our ways and use our words against us; for example, the name "Lakota Christian Academy" is at the very least contradictory. If you are a Lakota and you want to be Christian, then do not make that individual choice in the name of your people. Own it for yourself. One cannot be both because to call yourself Lakota is more than an issue of race, ethnicity, or biology (bloodline); it is to live and represent the entire spectrum of what our ancestors were—their beliefs; their sense of identity; their values, traditions, customs, and philosophies; and most importantly, how they applied all of these things to everyday life. And if one is fully aware of how cruel Christians were to our ancestors, how can any Lakota be one?

It is unavoidable to have and use the things of white mainstream culture, but that reality should not seduce us into being like the whites or adopting their thinking. A square house, a pickup truck, or a widescreen television should not cause us to forget our history, or obscure our ancestry. Any one of us who is racially Lakota has two choices: we can forsake our heritage and culture entirely or choose to actually be ethnically Lakota in every other respect. We can honor our values and traditions and observe our customs and live our spiritual beliefs. We can revere our children and our elderly. We can live the values that enabled our ancestors to be a family- and community-oriented society where helping others was a necessary privilege. We can teach our children and grandchildren the values that once made us a strong nation by being positive examples of respect and courtesy, among others things.

Furthermore, the values, social norms, and strong kinship system our ancestors used and kept in place is likely the best defense against drug and alcohol abuse, domestic violence, and suicides of our young people. The mainstream methods of combating these scourges have not worked effectively or consistently. Therefore, it is past the time to apply the strength and character of our ancestors, the core values of who we are—before we forget them entirely.

Sadly, there are those Lakota who think that the state of our culture today is a natural part of "progress," because change is a reality. If we could go back in time as observers and watch

Wounded Knee happen, or watch Harney's attack on Little Thunder's people at the Blue Water and see women and children being shot and mutilated and survivors taken captive, or watch Lakota children at Carlisle (or any boarding school) being forced to endure haircuts and take a white name, then we would probably have a different perspective. The colonizers whose ways some or many of us follow today committed those atrocities. Perhaps some would say we must forgive and forget. If so, that absolves the colonizers and makes it convenient for them, and it cruelly ignores the suffering of our ancestors. It is too convenient to say, "The past is the past and we cannot change it." That is true, of course. We cannot the change the past, but that should not be a rationale to forget it or ignore it. Some of us are hurt and insulted when someone else calls us a cruel name or gossips about us, and we rant about the pain of that insult on Facebook, and yet we cannot begin to imagine what it must have been like for Lakota women and children to be shot, raped, and eviscerated by Long Knives. For us not to acknowledge the pain and degradation suffered by those ancestors is to ignore their sacrifice, and their connection to us. Not to acknowledge them and their suffering is the same as saying they never existed, and that what they experienced—the horror of being raped or the physical pain they felt—does not matter. It mattered to them, it should matter to us.

We must and cannot cause Crazy Horse, and all the ancestors who clung steadfastly to being Lakota under the worst of circumstances, to weep any more than he, and they, already have. To forget who we are is to deny their humanity, to deny that they even existed. We are here because they lived. They had hopes and dreams, they loved life, they knew who they were, and they were proud of what they were. Those realities cannot and should not die under the wheels of "progress," trampled by axioms such as "The past is the past" or "We cannot live in the past" or by our unwillingness to embrace our own culture, heritage, and history.

I have written elsewhere about a small episode from my boyhood, about how my maternal grandfather, Albert Two Hawk, would take me on walks across the prairies or the meadows and thickets along the Little White River (which he called *Makizita Wakpa*, or Smoking Earth River). He would frequently pause and tell me to look back at the way we had come, and then we would move on. After many of these adventurous walks, I finally asked him why he told me to look back. "Because one day I will send you back on the trail by yourself," he said. "If you don't remember the way, you'll be lost."

For us Lakota, our past, our heritage, our ancestry is that path. Some of us, perhaps many, do not know it. Maybe that is one reason—or *the* reason—we seem to be lost today. In the physical, geographical, and territorial sense we obviously do not live as our ancestors did. Their families often had their lodges close or in the same area in the encampment or village, which served to maintain the closeness in the family dynamic. Today, our families are scattered across communities and housing projects miles apart on the reservation, or on other reservations, other parts of the state, or several states away. A remark often heard at funerals is, "The only time we see each other is at someone's funeral." It underlines the sad fact that the extended family, though it still exists, is not as close as it once was. We have lost that initial foundation of strength and cohesiveness—the family unit. That further weakens the *tiyospaye*, the community made up of extended families, which further weakens the tribe or nation as a whole.

A strong family was the basis for societal and tribal/national strength among us. In difficult times and circumstances, it was natural for families to band together to help mitigate a problem or overcome an obstacle, whether from within or from the outside. Now we seem more likely to band together *against* other families, usually over tribal politics or some mundane or innocuous reason more in keeping with schoolyard antics.

Assimilation is winning, and it will have achieved ultimate victory when the language is lost, when no one remembers the old stories, when Lakota children say their heroes are mythical movie characters or professional athletes, and when more of us say "Amen" at the end of a prayer rather than "*Mitakuye Oyasin.*" The fact of the matter is we are losing our way because we have forgotten who we are. We are past the tipping point and leaning down toward the side where we will one day be only biologically Lakota, claiming a lineage in smaller and smaller fractions of blood quantum, but we will have nothing ethnically or culturally.

That will certainly cause Crazy Horse and all the ancestors to weep.

Introduction

Before it was labeled North America, this continent was widely known as Turtle Island in the stories and lore of many of its indigenous inhabitants. A common creation story tells of a giant turtle rising from watery depths carrying the beginnings of life on its back, from which eventually grew the land and all its plants and animals. Interestingly enough, a satellite view of the continent does roughly show the shape of a turtle, its head is the Queen Elizabeth Islands region of what is now Canada, its left front foot is Alaska and the right is Baffin Island, and its back feet are the Baja and Florida peninsulas.

Life could not have been easy for the indigenous inhabitants of Turtle Island, which we now call North America. How many different groups of indigenous people were living here is unknown, as is the overall population, though estimates range from three to twenty million. But the fact of the matter is that our ancestors—and I am excluding Euro-Americans from the possessive "our"—lived on and in every part of this vast continent. They adapted to the climate, terrain, topography, weather, and flora and fauna. They built shelters from whatever materials were at hand, be it stone, wood, snow, and ice; plants such as bamboo and reeds; and animal hides. Their lifestyles were either nomadic or sedentary, depending on and influenced by the natural environment of the region they lived in. They hunted everything from squirrels to bison to whales; gathered nuts, berries, and seeds; fished with spears, nets, and traps; and did some planting and harvesting.

Life had to have been difficult, but it did not prevent our ancestors from thriving and forming cohesive societies with spiritual beliefs, codes of conduct and behavior, and societal roles for males and females. The foundation for spiritual beliefs was the reality of the natural environment, the cycles of the Earth and the seasons. Though specific beliefs, rituals, and ceremonies varied among the hundreds, if not thousands, of tribes and nations across Turtle Island, most acknowledged the connection to the Earth and shared a reverence for it—to the point that many called it Grandmother Earth, because she was the wise giver of life.

The foregoing is a common legacy shared by all descendants of Turtle Island's original inhabitants. The way each generation learned about those who had gone before was through the information and stories passed down to us, initially as children. And as each child listened to those stories, the seed of identity was planted and sense of self began to grow with it. By adolescence and young adulthood, those stories helped to solidify that identity, and we knew who we were and where we had come from. Sadly, this no longer happens.

Something came along and interrupted that ancient oral mechanism that was the conduit to how we became Inuit, or Penobscot, Oneida, Dine, Delaware, Creek, Makah, Ojibwe, and Lakota, and on, and on, and on…

I grew up in the 1940s and '50s, and I often wonder if my generation of Lakota children might have been the last to consistently hear those stories, in Lakota. I wonder that because I did not pass those stories on to my children in the same way my grandparents did for me, primarily because I lived a lifestyle much, much different than my grandparents had. But I do know one sobering reality. If we do not begin to learn who we really are as children from our parents and grandparents, other voices and other influences will push their way in. At the very least there will be confusion, but there can also be a total disconnect from who we are to the point where we feel lost and empty. I think we have now lost several generations of children to those other voices and to those other influences.

Crazy Horse Weeps is an essay, one that is divided into shorter essays. It is my attempt to discuss and understand the forces and processes that have caused us to lose much of our identity as Lakota people (and indigenous people in the broader context), and perhaps how to regain it. I take up this discussion not because I have any claim to knowledge, and even less to wisdom, but because as a Lakota person and a parent and grandparent I am concerned about the future and what it holds for Lakota people. Will we have a living language two generations from now? Will my great-grandchildren know their own true history? Will the colonizers win and finally *kill what is left of the Lakota*?

My hope and my prayer is for all Lakota children to begin to learn who they are at an early age, but not from non-Lakota teachers and school systems that teach the "winner's" version of history. I want them to learn from the parents, grandparents, and the community. Meanwhile, however, there are two to three generations who do not know their own history, or speak their language, or know the old stories. And the chances of those generations learning their history, learning to speak their language, and learning the old stories is practically nonexistent. The solution to that conundrum is neither easy nor immediate, but I think there is an answer, and it rests with our newest generations. We must begin to teach them while they are still young so that who and what they are will begin to find a niche or a foothold in the midst of all that is vying for their attention. Thus, we hope, they will grow into adulthood with a solid knowledge of Lakota culture and history and of speaking their own language. But they must also understand that there is a necessary—and yes, a sacred—duty to pass culture, history, and language on to their children and grandchildren. In other words, our culture, our history, our language must be *revived* in our children so that they grow up *knowing* and *understanding* and *living* who and what they are.

There are still first language Lakota speakers alive in our communities on every reservation. There are still Lakota people who know our cultural traditions and spiritual beliefs and the old stories of creation and morality. The sobering reality, however, is that most of these people are in their sixties, seventies, and eighties, and their journeys on Grandmother Earth are nearly finished. When they are gone, individually and collectively, what they know will go with them. We must learn as much as we can from these immeasurably valuable sources of information while they are still here. They are a key to reclaiming our culture and our identity. They must be involved if our children are to have any opportunity to learn who they are, so they can become Lakota in every sense of the word, and not stumble through life as a confused, biological version of who and what we once were.

The opinions expressed herein are my own, based on my experiences and the limited knowledge I have managed to gain. Of course they are largely influenced by the wisdom and insights and actions of previous generations, and by elder friends, younger friends, acquaintances, and other Native writers.

But the words are mine, and mine alone.

CRAZY HORSE WEEPS

Essays

Where Is the Village Now?

Although I did not grow up in the physical and social environment of a pre-reservation Lakota village, there is an enduring image in my mind because of my grandparents' stories and descriptions of them. And it is more than a visual image because their descriptions also brought to life the kind of social structure that existed to ensure the comfort and safety of families and community. According to them, it was the best environment for children to grow, and learn, and flourish.

Over the harsh winter months, villages were smaller and located close to water in areas sheltered from winter winds. Smaller villages meant fewer people, lodges, and horses, and that meant less of an impact on the natural environment. By late autumn enough meat had been laid in to last through the winter, so there was less of a need to hunt. A winter village could be anywhere from ten to twenty lodges and fifty to a hundred people—and usually more horses than people. However, winter villages were not located so far from each other that they were totally isolated. If weather permitted, people traveled to visit relatives and friends, or provide aid if necessary.

Once the weather broke in the spring, several villages came back together until late autumn or early winter. Then everything tripled or even quadrupled—30 to 40 lodges, a 150 to 200 people, and, of course, more horses. The summer, or good-weather villages relocated several times from spring to late autumn simply because a bigger village and more people and horses had a bigger impact on the environment. Frequent moves allowed the environment to restore itself.

There was one constant factor, however, with villages at any time of the year: each lodge occupied the same place. Lodges in winter villages were erected closer together and usually in a half-circle configuration, or sometimes in two. Since villages were composed of family units, or *tiwahe* (tee-wah-hay) that formed the community or *tiyospaye* (tee-yoh-shpah-yeh), it was important to reinforce the concept and function of families and the community. Therefore, lodges were placed accordingly, meaning, for example, a couple's married daughter and her family's lodge was adjacent to or directly behind them, and so on. So, while the locale of the village did change, the lodges were always in the same location.

Summer villages were usually arranged in circles, and concentric circles were often necessary, depending on the number of lodges. A very large village would therefore have three or four circles with an open area in the center. A council lodge was usually in the very center. Even in this arrangement, family lodges were located adjacent or close to one another. This design ensured an orderly arrangement, and it also enabled children to be close to their extended family, meaning maternal grandparents were always nearby, as were aunts and uncles and cousins.

Village arrangement was not random, and there were reasons for it, with most being practical. A circular village was easier to defend in the event of attack because it was not scattered randomly. Another important reason was to acknowledge the connection to the reality of the total environment, in this case the circle. In Lakota philosophy and reality, life is a circle because it begins with something new and helpless and concludes with something old and helpless. The stages are infancy, childhood, adulthood, and old age.

Villages were composed primarily of a few or many extended family units. In Lakota the word is *tiospaye*, meaning a community, or families living in groups, derived from *tiwahe*, meaning family, and *ospaye* (oh-shpah-yeh), meaning a group or band. The ex officio, if you will, leader or headman of the village, was usually the oldest patriarch in the sense that he was looked to for advice because he didn't have any day-to-day authority. He, in turn, would go to other elders in the community for their insight if and when a situation or problem arose.

Villages in the summer and winter existed to provide security and comfort for all occupants, but focused primarily on two groups—the young and the old. Those two groups were regarded as *oicihipi sni* (oh-ee-chee-hee-bee shnee) meaning "helpless ones" or "those who cannot help themselves." (Third syllable, first word is a plosive, and the *p* in the ending syllable is an integrated sound in that it is harder than the basic *p* and softer than the basic *b*.) This did not mean those two groups were in any way invalids, but they were regarded as the most vulnerable in the community. Therefore, in any emergency or crisis or prolonged activity, such as a village moving, it was expected that the adolescents and adults in the village would see first to the comfort and safety of "the helpless ones," the very young and the elderly. In this group were also those who were ill or infirm or otherwise debilitated in any way, temporarily or permanently.

Of course, the care of, concern for, and attention to "the helpless ones" occurred on a daily basis as well, not just in emergencies and crises. Members of the community provided whatever assistance the elderly might need, such as hauling water for them, or cooking, or taking down and putting up their lodges when the village moved. The responsibility fell on immediate family members but was consistently shared by everyone. Sons and grandsons of elderly couples, widows, and widowers would hunt for them, but so did all men in the village. This concern for and care of the elderly was not only because they were old and infirm, but also because they were the repository of knowledge and wisdom. While they were not able to contribute as much physically as they did as adults, their life experiences contributed just as much, or more, to the strength and well-being of the community. So they were relieved of their physical burdens to enable them to give of their knowledge and insight.

On the other spectrum of the "helpless ones" were the very young, from infants to (usually) twelve-year-olds. By the age of twelve, both girls and boys had learned basic skills that would enable them to survive on their own if it was necessary, and as they consistently demonstrated those skills to the satisfaction of their families, teachers, and mentors, they were relied on more and more as contributing members of the community. But until that point, the adolescents and adults looked out for their safety and well-being at all times, especially those from infancy to about five or six years of age.

At about five years of age, both girls and boys entered the period of their lives that involved learning physical skills and behavioral norms (or codes of conduct), and this was through a system of one teacher/mentor at a time, sometimes for each skill or norm. This training and learning process continued until about the age of sixteen, at which time the community had another young woman or young man who had learned all the necessary skills and knowledge to become an adult capable of contributing to the welfare of their families and the community. From that point, it was a matter of acquiring the experience.

For girls, the teachers/mentors were usually mothers and grandmothers—for one day or a particular skill, such as sewing, it might be Mom, and for another day or another skill, it might be Grandma. Other teacher/mentors were aunts and close family members. Learning began with the most basic skills and moved on to those more involved and intricate as the girl became older and/or demonstrated the requisite confidence and mastery. By the middle-teen years, girls were capable of caring for children and taking care of the dwelling and home, which included actually sewing together the buffalo-hide lodge coverings. They also learned the role of family nurturer, the behavior required for women, and the community's (and the larger society's) expectations of them as a women. They learned that their societal role as women was no less than the societal role for men. And in some ways it was more critical because women were the first teachers of all children, until about the age of five or six.

The process for boys was much the same, although the skills were obviously different, such as crafting weapons, horse training, tracking, and hand-to-hand combat. By the age of twelve, most boys were skilled hunters and thus could help provide for their families and others, and they could survive alone if necessary. By the time they were sixteen or seventeen, they had more than adequate skills as fighting men. Everything a boy learned was geared toward providing for and protecting home and family.

For both girls and boys, the validation of what they were taught came from the community at large, from the adults using the skills and demonstrating the behavior and values they espoused.

From infancy to young adulthood, everyone was taught by word and deed that he or she had a place in the group, beginning with the immediate family, to the extended family, and then to the community, society, and nation. For anyone to reach young adulthood without a sense of identity was a rare exception.

Everyone had a role in providing for the safety and welfare of children. The whole village raised the child.

Lakota children grew from a life of being indulged by parents, grandparents, and all adults into young men or women who knew their place in the society that nurtured and taught them. They were prepared to perpetuate the process that gave them their purpose and identity. Because of this process, aberrant behavior in adolescents and adults was the exception rather than a common occurrence. In the instances when it did occur, judgment by the community was swift, to the point of recompense for any injury that might have been caused.

Aberrant behavior was rare for two very strong reasons: everyone had a sense of place and purpose, and everyone knew who they were and where they came from. In other words, a strong sense of family, community, and identity is the best preventive for bad attitude and behavior. Or, to put it another way, how children were nurtured, raised, and taught was the foundation for strong families, strong communities, and a strong nation.

I was raised by grandparents who learned parenting skills from the way they were raised as well as by raising my mother and my uncle. For the most part, they indulged me when it came to where I played and what I tried to do. They showed me the things in my environment that could harm me, such as cactus needles, poison ivy, and mean-tempered badgers. They also showed me the things that could kill me, such as rattlesnakes and deep water. I learned early on that they knew what they were talking about when a badger chased me. I took refuge high in an oak tree, where I spent the better part of an afternoon until it finally went away. I stayed in the tree for a while longer because I remembered my grandmother telling me that a badger often circles back around on intruders to its territory. So when they told me that even grown men had drowned in the deep, fast current of the Little White River in the spring, I took it as the truth, because my grandmother was right about the badger.

Of course there were instances when I tested their patience, such as the time I tried to walk across an encrusted snowbank and broke through into deep snow—after my grandfather had told me that would happen. But for the most part, my childhood was idyllic because I was free to explore. As I grew more and more confident, my excursions took me farther and farther from our log house on the plateau above the river. Those years in my early childhood taught me independence and that solitude was a good thing. Of course I also had chores, such as gathering and hauling wood and keeping the bins by our stoves full, especially in the winter, and helping to haul water from the spring throughout the year. I have vivid memories of watching my grandfather walking behind a team of two large draft horses pulling a single bottom plow, and then a harrow to tear down the large dirt windrows. I can still see the plow blade shining like silver from the friction of tearing through an acre of soil. After the harrow made small furrows in the newly plowed dirt, we planted rows and rows of sweet corn, beans, and potatoes. One corner of the garden was reserved for pumpkins, squash, and watermelon. Of course, once the new plants emerged it was the continuous task of watering. This involved carrying buckets of water to the garden and slowly pouring it down each row. Then it was weeding and cultivating, and later picking potato bugs off the leaves.

We had a garden every year for the few years that we lived on the plateau above the Little White River, and there was a lot of work for all of us until everything was harvested and sold, stored, or canned. Not once did either of my grandparents tell me to help them. They always said, "We need your help," or, "It would be good to have your help." Back then, it did not matter how much or little I did—and because I was five, six, and seven when this occurred, I obviously could not do as much as either of them. Nevertheless, they always thanked and praised me for my efforts.

Looking back, even at this moment, the one reality that always resonates with me is that my grandparents did not interact with me the way they did simply because they were gentle souls. They were doing what the Lakota village did with the children in it, with patience and love and positive reinforcement. And even though that village no longer physically existed in the early 1950s, it was still there in a functional sense in much the same way as pre-reservation communities. Any time relatives came to visit—and most of them were of the same generation as my grandparents—uncles and aunts and other grandparents bolstered my self-esteem through positive interaction of their own. Of course, my grandparents never told of my missteps, only about the positive things I had done, and those remarks brought praise from my relatives and now and then with gifts as rewards. As I said, I did not live in a village with circles of lodges with relatives and families next door. Nevertheless, my grandparents and other relatives provided a glimpse into how a village raised a child.

My grandmother was born in 1900 and my grandfather in 1888, and their parents were born in the 1860s. My grandfather's father (my great-grandfather) was in his late teens when he fought at the Greasy Grass (Little Bighorn) in 1876. Afterward, the Lakota were moved from Fort Robinson to the Great Sioux Reservation (all of what is now western South Dakota) in 1877, for the most part into the areas where the current reservations are. They moved about in those areas until they took up permanent residence on allotments of land around 1910. As landowners they lived miles apart from one another, and the village, as a consistent cultural entity, was no more.

In spite of that, the function of the village as a community persisted because many people fifty years of age and older had experienced the physical, functional, and social dynamic of the village—the close-knit community of families—in their lifetimes, and carried that strong memory with them. So the *function* of the village was still operative for them and from that generation, especially insofar as children were concerned. Therefore, while my grandparents did not live in a village, their parents had. Consequently, my grandparents, as children, experienced the interaction with aunts, uncles, and the gamut of grandparents from both sides of the family. The only thing lacking was the physical proximity of families living in the same place.

The downside of the process was that this family dynamic occurred less and less frequently with each succeeding generation, and there were two reasons. First, the village, the mechanism for physical proximity of and for families, as in the pre-reservation era, was gone. The closeness afforded by the village had enabled almost daily and certainly regular interaction in and among families. Second, and most damaging, was the influence of white culture through the government, churches, and especially through boarding schools. Consequently, the *function* of the village—the extended family—diminished to the point of near extinction.

It is probably basic human nature that when someone or some force tries to take something away from us, we resist as much as we can. Thankfully, that was the case with indigenous people here on Turtle Island. In many ways, our culture went underground and became less obvious to the missionaries and the government, although they were insidious enough to recognize that reaction and took measures to mitigate it. On Lakota reservations in the late 1800s and early 1900s, for example, the government police were used to stop medicine men from conducting ceremonies. Those police forces employed Lakota men who, for the most part, informed on their own people, intentionally or not. It was common for those police, called the Indian Police, to arrest medicine men and confiscate their ceremonial objects. The most notorious use of Indian Police occurred when they were dispatched to arrest the Hunkpapa Lakota leader and medicine man, Sitting Bull, in December of 1890. That incident resulted in the murder of Sitting Bull by Indian Police, some of them his own relatives.

In spite of the government's and churches' efforts, Lakota people on all the reservations tenaciously clung to their culture and passed it on to the next generation. Because of that we still have a culture, albeit diminished and diluted significantly. One aspect of change that is arguably the most significant loss is the village and its function regarding the rearing, teaching, and mentoring of children. Today, Lakota parents are more influenced by white mainstream culture regarding the care, feeding, and rearing of their children, and one can only assume that in moments or periods of crises, Lakota parents are more likely to react much the same as Euro-American parents would. Although we are raising biologically identifiable Lakota children, we are not using ethnically Lakota methods and values. That is due, tragically, to our current reality of having forgotten who we are, and therefore the Lakota cultural approach to many aspects of life is no longer available to us. And the first to suffer the effects of that reality are our children.

We should not overlook the additional consequence of raising Lakota children who are learning non-Lakota values and behaviors. In their worldview, attitudes, and behavior, they are not Lakota. They are in every way, except biologically and racially, white people. I began to notice this dire effect in the late 1970s, in the last year I taught at a public school. Though the school was public, its student population was mostly Native; perhaps more than 90 percent of the Native students were Lakota.

I taught at both the junior and senior high school levels. Most noticeable in the senior high among the juniors and seniors, both Native and white, was the lack of respect and courtesy for adults, both verbally and behaviorally, though in fairness, it was not every student. At first I assumed the lack of respect and courtesy was due to the fact that, except for three or four, all the teachers in the junior and senior high school were white. However, some of the disrespect was also directed at me. There are, of course, many reasons for adolescents to display bad behavior toward adults, but I could not help but think that those sixteen- to eighteen-year-old Lakota students had little or no influence from a family knowledgeable of Lakota culture. In my four years of high school in the early 1960s I attended three public schools. Two had predominantly white student populations, though with about 20 percent Native, and one with a predominantly Native population. In each case all the teachers and administrators were white, and although all students had opinions about them, I would venture to say that 95 percent of our interaction with them was respectful and courteous—especially from us Native students.

Courtesy and respect, especially toward and for adults and the elderly, were the basis of family and societal interaction in Lakota culture. It was taught to children and reinforced by how adults interacted with one another in everyday life. Even when, beginning in the late 1870s, Lakota children were forcibly taken from their families and placed in government and parochial boarding schools and subjected to harsh treatment, many of them were at least courteous to their oppressors, even though they might not have respected them. This was how ingrained the values of respect and courtesy were in Lakota culture. An obvious factor in the erosion of those values was the influence of white people and their culture. In fact, Lakota parents today who are embracing the mainstream culture are usually not aware of the full scope of history after Lakota people submitted to white authority. Much of that story was, to say the least, of a powerful oppressor acting with impunity, enforcing not only policy but also individual prejudices on powerless victims—Lakota children and young people.

Oppressive attitudes and behavior have diminished over the decades, but not entirely. I recall an instance in high school involving a Bureau of Indian Affairs education coordinator, a middle-aged white male, who worked at the Rosebud Agency. He was driving me, along with two classmates, to an Indian education conference at a college in South Dakota. He told us that without an education we would never amount to anything because Indians had nothing going for them. It was far from being a benign remark. It felt like a scolding, meant to demean and belittle. None of us said a word because any amount of defiance from us would have been met with swift retribution. Further, the man had earlier made crude comments about a Lakota woman and her two daughters on a street corner, suggesting that the woman was pimping her daughters. Each of us knew the woman and nothing could have been further from the truth. I spent several weeks wallowing in guilt for not speaking up about the man's remark about the woman and her daughters. When I finally admitted it to my father, he reassured me that no amount of words from any Native person, young or old, would have made a difference. I learned later that my father confronted the man over the incident. The man, of course, denied saying anything to us or about the woman.

At any time, anywhere in the world, whenever one group of people operates from a position of strength and impunity, there are at least two reasons that group feels empowered: it knows its actions are sanctioned by others, or other groups fear it to the extent that they do and say nothing about any injustice that occurs. Christian missionaries and the US government operated from such a position of absolute power for more than a century on the northern plains among the Lakota and Dakota— not to mention among other indigenous tribes in other parts of the country. And on the other end of that spectrum is the oppression of the people living under the control of that absolute power. And further, the most vulnerable of the oppressed are the children and young people because of one elemental and dreadful tool of the oppressor: to change a culture, prevent the children from learning it. This is still occurring for the Lakota and other indigenous people, and right under our noses.

Even back in elementary school, history was my favorite subject. This was due in no small part to the stories I had heard from my grandparents and other elders about Lakota history. The only problem was that it was not a yearlong subject in the lower elementary grades. At one of the schools I attended, I learned about South Dakota history. If memory serves, the textbook was just over a hundred pages long and was mostly about the settlers who came to the plains with their plows and cattle and turned wilderness into civilization. My ancestors were mentioned on no more than five or six pages, and then only in terms of "They were here and now they live on reservations." That certainly did not coincide with what I had learned from my grandparents. In sixth grade, the teacher talked about the Battle of the Little Bighorn, and that was the first time I heard it referred to something other than the Greasy Grass Fight. When the teacher went on at length about the heroic "Last Stand" of General George Custer, it was the first time I had heard his name associated with the story. Furthermore, the version she told differed from the story my great-grandfather, who was there as a combatant, had told his son, my grandfather, who in turn told it to me. There was no prolonged last stand. So I raised my hand, one of the few times I did, and timidly told what my grandfather had told me. Although she listened patiently, the teacher then told me we should stick with the real story—that being the heroic version.

The obvious fact here is that Lakota and Dakota history, as its own subject or course, was not taught at all in any school—public, parochial, or government. And when they were taught, my ancestors were labeled as obstacles to progress and civilization who eventually became wards of the government. Throughout my entire elementary and high school experience, Native history was never any more than a passing mention, and one that was never very flattering.

About fifteen years ago, a Native colleague of mine who was teaching at a university in Sioux Falls asked me to talk to one of her classes. The subject she taught was Native history, a course that was required for teacher recertification. After my remarks, one of the students—a white high school teacher, as I recall—asked if I thought it would be fair if a white history course were taught as well. My response was to remind her that the entire educational system in this country, much less South Dakota, was geared toward white culture. I pointed out to her that her history—white history—was a required subject, from elementary school to college, and that Native history was usually only generally and briefly mentioned, and if it was offered, it was as an elective.

During the past five years, I have had the privilege of visiting at length with several people, mostly Lakota and Dakota women, about the issues related to the future of Lakota and Dakota children and young people. In the group were a college president, an activist, a journalist, a social worker, and a counselor. All of them have worked or are working on a reservation, with organizations and institutions serving Lakota youth, tribal government, and the federal government, and each was a parent and a grandparent.

The topic of the conversations was how best to ensure the future for Native youth, and where the shortcomings were in the various organizations and entities, both state and tribal, whose mission was to serve, enable, assist, and empower them. The insights they shared were, of course, from their own personal and professional experiences and philosophies. They were straightforward, heartfelt, hopeful, and sometimes brutally honest. Following is a summary of their comments and insights:

- Education is key, but in addition to courses required for a given major or field of study, Native students should be encouraged to choose electives that will teach them their own history, culture, language, and other issues relevant to their communities and reservations.

- Institutions of learning from high school to college should offer history, culture, and language courses taught, wherever possible, by Native teachers and professors.

- Lakota and Dakota history should be taught honestly in public schools and especially in Native-controlled schools and Native colleges and universities.

- First language Lakota and Dakota speakers should be identified and used as expert resources by Native-controlled schools and colleges.

- Tribal governments should take a more proactive role in ensuring that regulations and laws intended to help and protect Lakota and Dakota children and young people, such as the Indian Child Welfare Act, be fairly administered.

- That identity is critical to personal growth and development for Lakota and Dakota children, and young people should be the first consideration for any adult, Native or non-Native, who works with or provides any service to Lakota and Dakota children and young people.

- Cultural awareness and sensitivity training should be developed and mandated for any adult, Native or non-Native, who works with or provides any service to Lakota and Dakota children and young people, including those employed by tribal, county, state, and federal programs.

- The state Department of Social Services should only be allowed to take Lakota and Dakota children from their homes and families in consultation with tribal social service programs, and first priority is placement with Lakota and Dakota foster families before white families are ever considered, as some or many white foster parents take in Native children primarily as a source of income, and some or many lack the cultural knowledge to provide a supportive environment. In addition, there are concerns because of stories of verbal, physical, and sexual abuse suffered by Native children.

- Tribal and state social service programs should continuously recruit eligible Lakota and Dakota families to be foster parents and provide necessary training.

Since missionaries first came to the reservations and into Lakota and Dakota communities, and since the first Lakota and Dakota children were torn from their mothers' arms and taken to boarding schools, there has been a war to indoctrinate each new Lakota and Dakota generation. And the focus of that indoctrination has been the children. It began with stripping away their Lakota and Dakota names and then forbidding them to speak their language—the core of their identity. This is the American way—tear down the old and reconstruct and reshape it into something acceptable to them. Consequently, each generation's sense of individual and ethnic identity was diminished, but so was their ability to pass it on to their children. That there is still a Lakota (and Dakota) culture today is nothing short of a miracle, considering what previous generations had to endure at the hands of those whose express purpose was to destroy it.

My father was in the seventh grade at the Rosebud Boarding School when he was punished for speaking Lakota on campus. He was made to kneel on a two-by-four in front of the principal's office for an entire afternoon. When he was caught the second time, the consequence was more severe. He was, more or less, hung from a basement water pipe by his thumbs, with a cord around each thumb and over the pipe. To prevent his thumbs from dislocating, he had to stand on his tiptoes, which he did until his calf muscles cramped. At that point, he said, he jumped up and grabbed the pipe and hung from it until someone came down to check on him. This was in 1936, not in the late 1800s.

A relative of mine told how she was punished. The teacher (I believe she said a nun) put her inside a dark, hot, stifling closet and locked the door. She said the only light and cool air came in from the bottom of the door where there was perhaps a quarter inch of space. She had to lie prone on the floor to put her mouth close to that space in order to get fresh air and see some light. This was in the early 1950s, not in the late 1800s.

My father said the punishment he received was humiliating and physically very painful, but other children were punished far worse for the same offense.

In most instances like these, the consequences of speaking Lakota were severe, but the consequences of the punishment ignited a spark of resolve, an urge to resist and persist. That is why there is still a Lakota and Dakota culture today. Unfortunately, most Native young people today do not hear these stories from those who endured the punishment, or if they do hear them, they cannot relate. Too often for young people, those types of stories are "ancient history" with no bearing on their lives.

Not enough has been written or said about the government and parochial boarding school era and its individual toll on Lakota and Dakota children. Obviously, there are some who say it was not as bad for them, but I believe there are more who have indicated otherwise, from unpleasant experiences to outright physical and sexual abuse. It does not and should not matter whether *any* type of abuse happened to only a few or to (I suspect) many, whether it happened in only a few instances or (I suspect) hundreds of times—it is unconscionable and inexcusable. Whether it is unforgivable or not is a determination that can be made only by those who suffered the abuse.

The boarding school era occurred because the government and the Catholic Church operated from a position of absolute impunity and the perspective of the God-given right and responsibility to change and improve us as Lakota and Dakota people—to educate us and to bring us to their god because they believed we were racially and otherwise inferior to white people in every way. Perhaps it is difficult, if not impossible, to quantify to what extent they destroyed our culture and obfuscated our history, but if those boarding schools had continued for another generation or two, the possible, and perhaps probable, unfathomable consequence would be an entire nation that was only *biologically* Lakota and Dakota. What we do need to understand as Lakota and Dakota people is that *that was exactly what the government and Catholic Church wanted to do.*

We current versions and generations of Lakota and Dakota people should never forget the sacrifices made and suffering endured by our ancestors for the simple fact that they were Lakota and Dakota. They fought and died at the Greasy Grass to defend themselves and their nation and culture. In my opinion, those generations of Lakota and Dakota children who experienced the boarding schools—be it on the reservations or in Carlisle, Pennsylvania, or wherever they were sent—and outwardly or inwardly resisted and were punished and abused simply for being Lakota and Dakota, also fought to defend their culture. And although their battle was strung out over generations and their victory was not entirely decisive, they were victorious nonetheless—because we still have a culture and some sense of who we are. For at least those reasons and because those Lakota and Dakota people, the warriors (both men and women) of Greasy Grass and the boarding school students, were our ancestors, our relatives, we must never regard what they did as simply "ancient history" or something not connected to us. They were real flesh-and-blood people with weaknesses and strengths, families, and hopes and dreams—just as we are in the here and now. And we owe them, at the very least, the courtesy of learning and remembering what they did.

No matter how difficult our history has been, especially since Europeans and Euro-Americans came into our lands and our lives, we must never forget it or allow anyone else to tell it for us or to us. There are lessons for us Lakota and Dakota people in that history, from the broad and necessary perspectives of what *to* do and what *not* to do. For me, one lesson is for us never to forget who we are, and then to do everything in our power and within our ability to ensure that our culture and our nation are not further diminished. In order for us to accomplish both of those goals, our collective focus must be on teaching each new generation of Lakota and Dakota children their history and their culture.

In my opinion, the only lesson the mainstream white culture has learned from their history with us is that they failed, because we are still here. When our ancestors tried desperately to achieve peaceful change through prayer and dancing during the Ghost Dance era, the US government assumed it would lead to an armed uprising and, fearing for their lives and property, quashed it with guns and bullets. When we—along with members of other Native tribes—peacefully protested the Dakota Access Pipeline, a threat to the well-being of the environment that we all share, they came with guns, tear gas, and attack dogs. If they had learned anything, it was far from remorse for their misdeeds of the past, which includes massacres and the abuse of children.

The hard lesson we must pass on to our children and grandchildren is that there is a price for being Lakota and Dakota, as the colonizer has doubled down on its attitude of Manifest Destiny. Why else would a white male candidate for the US House of Representatives from South Dakota in 2018 state boldly that it is time to terminate reservations? He is another in a long line of "Indian Fighters" of the same ilk that rode into the valley of the Greasy Grass or opened fire on women and children at Wounded Knee in 1890. A list that includes a school board that will not allow Lakota honoring songs for Lakota students at a public high school graduation; a white man who verbally and physically abused Lakota school children at a public event, and the white judge that set the abuser free; white basketball referees who make questionable calls against Lakota basketball players competing against white teams; white small-town basketball fans who hurl racial epithets when a high school basketball team with Lakota players wins the state championship. Lakota children experienced all of these situations and incidents, and these are far from isolated events.

Is there hope for something better? Of course there is, and it abides in Lakota and Dakota families—parents, grandparents, aunts, and uncles—taking an active role in preparing their children and grandchildren and nieces and nephews to survive and thrive in a world controlled by the colonizer. And that means nothing less than giving them a strong sense of their individual and cultural identity. For this to happen, Lakota and Dakota people must revive, or relearn if necessary, the function of the extended family in all of our communities, both reservation and urban. Until that becomes a consistent functional reality, Lakota and Dakota children will continue to be at risk.

A few years ago, a Native woman living and working on her home reservation in South Dakota related a story of an early morning incident that occurred on her way to work. She saw a teenage boy walking along the road, but not in the direction of the school. He accepted her offer of a ride when she stopped, though it was obvious he was not prepared to go to school. He was unkempt and was clearly upset or unhappy. She knew the boy and of his difficult family situation, so she suspected something was awry. After a few questions, which he answered hesitantly, the boy broke down. To her surprise and shock he admitted he had been on his way to find a tree to hang himself.

Although he was not himself, this teenage boy's family was heavily into drugs and alcohol. He and his siblings were subjected to their parents' substance abuse on almost a daily basis, forcing the children to take care of themselves, meaning cooking their own meals and taking care of household responsibilities such as finding money for utility bills and rent. The children were undernourished and not performing well in school.

After years of frustration, uncertainty, and hopelessness, and with no apparent chance for circumstances to improve, and no help in sight, the boy sought to bring an end to his misery in the only way he could—by deciding to end his life.

Fortunately, the kind and caring woman's fortuitous offer of a ride was the beginning of an intervention. The boy did not hang himself and assistance from tribal and state social services began a process of mitigation for him and his siblings. But the unseen part of this story is that it is not an isolated incident.

On any given morning, on any of the reservations in what is now the state of South Dakota, Lakota and Dakota children and young people wake up to an uncertain future. Some days—hopefully most—will turn out well, in that there will be food, shelter, warmth, good health, and good and caring adults in their lives. In the cold and harsh reality of life, however, that is not always the case because those basic necessities are not always available all together, all the time. And there are too many instances when none of them are available at all. There are any number of organizations and agencies that crank out statistics to indicate how many Lakota and Dakota children wake up to that uncertain future, but suffice to say that even one child or young person going without is one too many.

Alcohol has been a scourge on the Lakota people, to put it mildly. Rare is the Lakota family on any reservation that it has not touched, directly or indirectly. In my hometown, a young man barely past thirty years of age was buried recently because he literally drank himself to death. Alcohol abuse from his early teenage years finally destroyed his liver. Again, this is not an isolated incident. Furthermore, every kind of illegal drug that found its way into mainstream American society—LSD, crack cocaine, heroin, and crystal meth, among others—has wreaked havoc on reservations. A drive though any housing project on my home reservation, as well as others, would reveal many unoccupied and boarded-up houses. Most such houses are where meth was cooked. And if it was cooked, it was distributed and used. At this point in time, methamphetamine use is rampant on every reservation in this state, as it is in the mainstream society's small towns, cities, and rural communities. And yet I do not see the efforts to confront and battle this tragic and destructive epidemic on the same level as the swiftness with which it is claiming victims through addiction and destruction of families. Indeed, perhaps the frightening reality is that we do not know how to fight it. And if that's the case, ignorance is not bliss. Ignorance is an ally to this epidemic.

Military funding in the US budget has increased outrageously under the current administration—this to fight mostly imaginary enemies said to be out to destroy America. While those imaginary enemies are destroying common sense based on the fear-mongering of self-serving politicians adept at fanning the flames of misguided patriotism, ethnocentrism, and white nationalism, a real enemy is destroying all of us from within: methamphetamine. Yet billions of dollars are not being allocated to fight that enemy.

On a tribal level, insofar as current tribal governments are concerned, the scourge of meth has not been, nor is it being, addressed consistently—except perhaps to acknowledge that it is indeed a problem. Acknowledgment alone does not and will not begin to solve the problem. An effective plan and effective leadership must be a large part of the solution.

One of the ancient Lakota edicts of defeating an enemy was to know it intimately. It is critical for us—as parents, grandparents, and community members—to know all we can about this enemy called meth, to know its ugly realities, to know how it destroys sons, daughters, mothers, fathers, and friends, and to inform every living soul about it. Meth is far from an ordinary enemy; this is one that will kill us all in one way or another if left unchecked—as has been the case thus far. Anyone, any organization, any entity that works or is involved with families, and especially young people, must be a consistent conduit of information about meth.

Just over two years ago I attended a monthly meeting of my home community on the Rosebud. As is unfortunately the case with most Lakota communities, only a dozen people were in attendance, which was even more unfortunate because of the excellent presentation given by a young woman from the tribal social services program. She talked about the methamphetamine epidemic on the reservation, which included concise and graphic and totally frightening insights into the effects addiction, not only on the user (or abuser) but on family as well.

The physical effects of meth are ugly, to say the least, and what I heard in that presentation needs to be heard by every adult, by every parent and grandparent. Coincidentally—or perhaps not—I happened to meet a young acquaintance after ten years. Ten years ago, in her mid-twenties, she had achieved her goal of graduating with a teaching degree. Then she was a beautiful young mother. Two years ago she looked as though she had aged twenty hard years. She was seriously underweight, and she was pale with blotches on what had been a flawless complexion. I was shocked at her appearance, to say the least. Later, a mutual friend informed me that the young woman was hooked on meth, and had lost her daughter, her husband, and her job.

There are too many stories like this, and it tragically validated one remark made by the tribal social worker in her presentation: "Meth addiction is nearly impossible to recover from." We hope that this is not always the case, but while I'm certain they are out there, I have not heard many stories of successful recovery from meth addiction.

Meth is the new scourge, it is our enemy, and perhaps most of us will never learn how and why it is so utterly destructive. But we do not need scientific analysis to know that it destroys anyone who uses it; it destroys their families, and it is destroying entire communities. That is the reality of this enemy, and unless we as families and communities meet it head-on, it will certainly destroy our Native culture long before assimilation will.

And this is but a small part of our reality.

To Influence the Actions and Attitudes of Others

To my way of thinking, the words *reservation* and *economy* together are the classic oxymoron. And always the glaring statistic waved as the banner of tribal failure is the unemployment rate that hovers, on any reservation, around 80 percent. The first assumption made, likely especially by white readers, is that Lakota people (or Natives in general) are unwilling to work. The hidden reality is that there are not enough jobs on any reservation to go around. Any nonfederal or nontribal employer on and around a reservation is most likely to hire qualified non-Natives/whites first, and even underqualified non-Natives/whites before qualified Natives. And poverty-stricken Natives and whites compete for the few minimum wage jobs available, usually seasonal or menial.

To survive economically and physically on any reservation requires a certain amount of toughness bolstered by a generous dose of stubbornness. People are forced to use any resource available, such as food stamps and welfare, and do odd jobs in order to provide for family, pay rent and utilities, afford a car and school clothes, and all the basic necessities of life. Suffice to say Native people do work at many kinds of jobs on and around the reservations, from basic labor to professional positions. Still, the average annual income is approximately $17,000, with 20 percent of families at $5,000 or below.

All of the foregoing are sobering realities that have existed
for many decades.

There are, of course, many more aspects to life on any reservation beyond health, education, and the economy. As far as
I am concerned, those factors have the most immediate and
enduring impact on Lakota lives, day in and day out, year in
and year out. And these are the factors that have continually
stymied Lakota governments—tribal councils and presidents/
chairpeople—the most. One only has to learn how long the
unemployment rate on reservations has hovered around 80 percent to understand the apparent inability of tribal governments
to change it. All of this leads us to the topic of reservation-era
Lakota leaders and leadership.

Pre-reservation Lakota leadership (see page 62) arguably continued to function, to varying degrees of effectiveness, until
the modern tribal councils were in place, after the US Congress passed the 1934 Indian Reorganization Act, or IRA. Many
tribes complied with the provisions of the act and formed governments modeled after the US system of legislative, executive,
and judicial branches. Thus elected tribal councils and presidents
or chairpeople became the core of the new system, followed by
tribal courts. Those tribes that rejected the IRA government
use a general council system instead, in which adult enrolled
tribal members are the council, although in those instances the
top officials—president or chair, vice president, and so on—are
elected at large.

Even after the Lakota acquiesced to white authority and
lived under their control at Fort Robinson (in what is now northwestern Nebraska), many of the people looked to the established
leaders for guidance, those that had risen to leadership in the
old way. The US government's Indian Bureau, or the Bureau

of Indian Affairs (BIA), tried to circumvent this by appointing "agency chiefs." After the Oglala Lakota leader Crazy Horse came to Fort Robinson in May of 1877, and Sitting Bull returned from Canada in 1881 and surrendered to white authority at Fort Union in the North, the Lakota people were even more inclined to rely on the established leaders and the old leadership system. After Crazy Horse was killed in September of 1877, the US government moved the Lakota into separate areas on the "Great Sioux Reservation," as so delineated in the 1868 Fort Laramie Treaty. That reservation was the entire western half of the current state of South Dakota, beginning at the Missouri River. In those years, though the white authority tightened their control through their Indian agents and appointed agency chiefs, it was the old leaders that the people still looked to for guidance. It was during the years after 1877 that the present locations of the reservations became permanent, as did the English names of those places and the people that lived on them, such as the Rosebud Sioux, the Standing Rock Sioux, and so on.

Even after the provisions of the 1934 IRA were implemented on the reservations, the old leadership hierarchy more or less remained in place, mainly because the Lakota, at least most of them, were not so quick to put their trust in anything to do with white people.

But eventually it was evident that the new system was here to stay, and when elections were conducted the people selected those who were leaders already or had the right character and temperament and experience for leadership—as in the old days. There was an inherent flaw in the new system, however, because the minimum age to stand for election to most tribal councils was twenty-five. Sooner rather than later, younger and younger men stood for election and begin to win seats on the councils.

One of the qualities desired in leaders in the pre-reservation era was experience and a record of achievement on behalf of the people. But in the new era of IRA councils, that was not the case. With each election, beginning in the late 1940s, the average age of tribal councils became younger, and with younger people comes less experience. Gone, of course, were the days of the hunter and warrior; there was no longer any way to learn under the tutelage of older and experienced men and develop a record of achievement. The experience and knowledge of the younger elected council representatives did not go back beyond the time the mantle of white authority came into Lakota life. There was no more need to provide for the people as a hunter, and certainly no more opportunities to protect the people as a warrior of old. The worldview and experiential base of the new, younger leaders was instead predominantly influenced by white society. And that has been increasingly the case ever since those early days of tribal councils.

Because we Lakota are now even more part of a global community, obviously because of technology and the internet, it is critically necessary for our leaders to be knowledgeable of two worlds: the reservation and the world outside of it.

The reservations are our homelands. They are exterior borders and a land base, albeit a shrinking one, and they have Native populations ethnically different from the rest of mainstream society. Since the implementation of the Dawes Severalty Act of 1887, which really did not begin to take effect until 1910, white people have been part of the population inside those exterior borders. The Dawes Act opened up surplus reservation lands to white homesteading, and there were, if you will, three groups of whites living inside the reservations. In the first group were those who, since the inception of reservations in South Dakota (actually before South Dakota became a state), were employed by the Bureau of Indian Affairs. The second group was the missionaries, especially the Catholics who were given land to establish schools. Third were the homesteaders, who squatted on surplus Indian lands, and traders who sought to make a living off of Indians. So, almost from the beginning, we have had to share our homeland with white people, and the relationship has not been convivial.

The current makeup of our homelands, the reservations, is confusingly complex because of land ownership within exterior borders. White land ownership within reservations in South Dakota is significant. This affects licensure of hunting and fishing, civil and criminal jurisdiction, and tribal sovereignty. Lakota children in public schools, racism, and a largely adversarial relationship with the state of South Dakota add to the complexity. These roiling circumstances, and others, make up the environment in which Lakota people must exist and at least try to continue as a viable culture. And it is these circumstances that affect our children because they are the ones impacted most by the shortcomings and mistakes of the society and community they live in, on and off the reservations.

Modern Lakota tribal governments have been faced with these circumstances for decades, and the situation has not improved under their watch. Admittedly, they can only take on part of the problem solving, as many of the problems were and are caused by the attitudes and actions of white America—past and present—as well as the actions, attitudes, and policies of the state of South Dakota and its officials, and even more so the US government. Any progress we have made toward improving circumstances is a consequence of occasional good tribal leadership, a bit of luck, and some degree of cooperation from white people, be it individuals or county governments, school boards, or state and federal entities. While we have been occasionally blessed with good Native leaders, we have also had our share of inept tribal councils, presidents, and chairs—perhaps more often than not.

Tribal councils and tribal presidents need to be aware of all of the circumstances, forces, and influences both from within and beyond reservation borders that have and will affect the lives of tribal members, and must continually inform and educate themselves. Furthermore, they must not forget or ignore the fact that they work for the people. On my home reservation, those who are elected to and serve on the tribal council are called community representatives.

A representative form of government is a simple process; the people are to be represented by those who are elected to do so. The people's needs, ideas, and opinions should be the driving force in the government. Unfortunately, perhaps tragically, this does not happen consistently. Whereas the community representatives should simply be conduits from the community to the tribal council, they often change or ignore their constituents' words, wishes, and opinions simply because they think they know better, or because what constituents want does not fit with the representatives' personal agenda. Too often, a newly elected community representative considers his or her office a prize to be exploited for personal gain rather than a responsibility to the community, and/or that they are magically imbued or "dusted" with wisdom the second they take the oath of office. This latter predicament, however, is obviously not restricted to tribal politicians. Frankly, it is likely more rampant across the country at the city council, county commissioner, state legislature, and US congressional levels.

Part of the problem is that we associate the word *politician* with the word *leader,* which is like trying to mix oil and water. Since the American system of government is inextricably linked to capitalism, the greed for money and power is the same. That system, from towns and cities to the "hallowed" halls of Congress, is filled with politicians whose sense of responsibility to their constituency comes in a distant second to just about everything else. Unfortunately, some of us in Indian country have learned that aspect of "being like white men" all too well.

Tragically, ineffectual leadership in this country is not just fodder for gossip and quasi-analytical pundits. It affects us all. In 2019, all we need do is take a hard look at the changes this country's current president is secretly mandating behind the scenes, obviously goaded on by the Christian conservatives hell-bent on pushing their agendas.

Ineffective leadership at the tribal level in Indian country means that the status quo continues—sky-high unemployment, epidemics of meth abuse, and so on. In the recent past we have lost more land and further eroded our sovereignty because weak and ineffectual tribal presidents were more eager to please the feds and line their own pockets. And unless those grievous actions are corrected, the consequences will be borne by our grandchildren and great-grandchildren. And at the rate we are *not* teaching them their history and *not* inculcating them with their culture—especially how pre-reservation Lakota leadership was effective—they will not be equipped to understand either of them and will thus be unable to find the right solutions.

Our so-called leaders suffer from the same shortcomings of elected officeholders in white mainstream society—they do not represent their people, those who elected them to office. Of course, in a cruelly convoluted example of that, Donald Trump represents the irresponsible, reprehensible, ethnocentric, and selfish attitudes of some 62 million white Americans. This is likely the only time in white American history it has happened, and it serves the dark side of American society.

Yesterday's Hero

First impressions, it is said, are important and set the tone for the interactions or judgments that follow. With that in mind, consider how the nineteenth-century Lakota warrior has been portrayed, primarily by non-Native observers. Circumstances during which those observations were made were usually not positive, ranging from the possibility of clash and conflict to outright confrontations. White observers in those situations were mostly male, with the exception of the wagon train era from the mid-1840s to the mid-1860s, when white families were involved. Regardless, first impressions taken by white people were typically negative. *Fierce, dirty, warlike, savage, bloodthirsty*, and a variety of other uncomplimentary labels were common. And those labels were, to a certain extent, influenced by attitudes toward Natives east of the Mississippi River. By the time of the 1804 Lewis and Clark Discovery Expedition, many of the eastern tribes had been subjugated, and the classic "conqueror" mentality was directed at those perceived to have been conquered. The lore of white "conquest" of the eastern woodlands was rife with the labels later applied to the Natives west of the Mississippi River. So the opinions of and attitudes toward western Native people were already in place before many whites had set foot into those territories, and the first sighting of a Lakota male mounted on a horse with weapons in his hand affirmed all the presumptions.

By that time the attitude of Manifest Destiny was firmly in place, hence Euro-Americans regarded any Native person or group that even appeared on a distant horizon as an impediment to progress. All of these factors, and likely more, precluded white people from regarding that dark-skinned Lakota male as human.

Ironically, that Lakota male mounted on a horse and bearing weapons was displaying a basic human trait—he was protecting his family and all that he held dear. He was trained and influenced to do that because being a protector was one of two societal roles fulfilled by Lakota males. The other was to be a provider.

The whites who stared suspiciously and fearfully at the man on horseback perceived him only as a threat to *their* safety and well-being, never for a moment considering that he regarded them in the same way. Their ingrained sense of Manifest Destiny obfuscated the reality that they were the strangers and they were encroaching on his homeland.

The homelands of the Lakota ranged west from the Missouri River to the foothills of the Big Horn Mountains, and north from the Niobrara and North Platte Rivers to the Yellowstone River—an area larger than many European countries at the time. Within this territory were seven bands or groups encompassing the Lakota, with a population of 15,000 to 20,000 by the mid-1800s. (The Dakota were east of the Missouri.) And those seven groups lived in hundreds of village scattered within their own distinct territories. Our ancestors had evolved into nomadic hunters soon after they arrived on the northern plains, even before the arrival of the horse. When horses arrived, the lifestyle was enhanced and territories expanded. Within that nomadic lifestyle was a cohesive society that had evolved for countless generations, with strong societal norms based on family and community.

These realities were not evident, of course, to the first white people who came into Lakota territories. The Lakota were judged largely by comparison to white culture and were found wanting simply because they were not the same, lacked the technology Europeans and Euro-Americans had, did not worship the same god, and lived in concert with the natural environment instead of in conflict with it as whites did.

When a white person laid eyes on that Lakota man on a horse with weapons in hand, their immediate reaction was most likely fear. Fear based on ignorance, misinformation, and negative attitudes toward people of color was already part of white ethnocentrism. Fear based on the assumption that the man on a horse was there to attack them. In reality, that man was there to protect his family, his village, and his way of life, *from* them.

Lakota males were taught to be providers and protectors. And they fulfilled their roles so well that the Lakota nation, in confederation with the Dakota and Nakota, became the strongest on the northern plains. The societal roles of providers and protectors can be accurately labeled as hunter/warrior. As hunters they provided food and the materials for shelter and clothing. As warriors they provided security for their families and villages. Within the broad label of hunters and warriors, they were also sons, husbands, fathers, uncles, and grandfathers, not to mention teachers and mentors, trackers, and bow-and-arrow makers. The philosophy that underscored all of these roles was that families came first. In other words, the hunter hunted to provide meat; animal hides for clothing, robes, and coverings for the lodge; and all the material resources required for everyday life and comfort. As the warrior, they stood between any threat—large or small—and the families in the village. But what historians and sociologists often overlook is that those responsibilities coincided with being fathers, uncles, and grandfathers, and as such they were fiercely protective of the *tiospaye*, the community made of extended families. They were taught to take care of and protect women, children, and the elderly.

It was a common practice for men leading warriors into battle to remind them to "remember the helpless ones." That was the basic reason for being a warrior. Though Lakota warriors were fierce in battle, they were also gentle and doting fathers, but stern when necessary, and their parenting responsibilities extended into their roles as uncles and grandfathers. Not every man was the best possible father or uncle or grandfather, of course—as is the case across time, cultures, and societies the world over—but we can say with certainty that most of them did their best.

It was the father as a hunter who spent the majority of his time pursuing and harvesting game animals, large and small, for days at a time and often at great distances away from his family. It should be noted that many men also provided for the elderly and widows who had no one to hunt for them. Lakota men took care of their families.

Lakota women obviously did the same, not as hunters but rather as nurturers and the first teachers of children. It was said that Lakota boys learned the ways of the hunter/warrior from their fathers, uncles, and grandfathers but learned courage and compassion from their mothers, aunts, and grandmothers.

Under this arrangement, every boy was left to his mother, older sisters, aunts, and grandmothers until about the age of five or six. Therefore, his first and most important influence and lessons came from women. At this point, although they continued to receive further learning and lessons from females, each boy began the intensive process of learning from his father, uncles, older brothers, and grandfathers the necessary and practical lessons of being the hunter and warrior. As it did for girls, the system depended on a one-on-one mentoring approach; essentially one mentor/teacher at a time. Although boys played with other boys, as girls played with other girls, rarely were they brought together in a group-learning environment. The only activity that could be considered consistent group learning was listening to stories, usually told by the elderly—the grandparents in the village/community hierarchy. Therefore, there was nothing like the European/Euro-American method of several children entrusted to one teacher who imparted basic lessons on behalf of parents. In pre-reservation Lakota society, in both the village and community, every adult was a teacher and mentor, whether the teaching moment was brief or extended, because practical skills, proper behavior, and respectful and courteous conduct were essential to the harmony and well-being of the family and the community.

And importantly, for boys, their early and continued association with women taught them to understand the roles of women in their lives, in the family dynamic, and in the extended family and community around them. This was the basis for a lifelong respect for women.

No society, no culture, no nation anywhere—past or present—was or is perfect. And throughout the history of humankind, nations have been known by characteristics or accomplishments that have set them apart, and that are the basis for their identities, their fame, or their notoriety. Usually first on that list was imperialism, the drive to conquer territory and subjugate other peoples, primarily for control, riches, and resources. The Mongols, Romans, and several European nations are in this category—the British, French, Spanish, and Dutch. Every conquering group or society was driven by one need: materialism, and controlling each group or society was either an autocracy or an oligarchy. And a countless number of those societies, cultures, and nations flourished and then were lost or diminished, either by their own mistakes or being overwhelmed by others. Human history is filled with such stories, and most of them will never be known. What is too frequently overlooked is a consequence of one group being overwhelmed by another, and that is *absorption*. However else being overwhelmed is described, either as "conquered" or "dominated" or in some other way, the cultural consequence is loss, as many of us contemporary Natives are painfully aware. We were absorbed (and still are) by the Euro-American mainstream, and the most devastating losses are the tenets, norms, and values that were the foundations of our cultures and societies. In my opinion, one of the most culturally debilitating losses for us Lakota is the societal role of the male—that of the provider and protector, or the hunter and warrior.

One of the first symbolic and necessary gestures (according to the army) demanded of Lakota men when they arrived to surrender at Camp Robinson in the mid- to late 1860s, in what is now northwestern Nebraska, was to relinquish their guns and horses. A gun (or a weapon) and a horse were the very symbols of the Lakota hunter-warrior, and without them he lost a part of his personal identity, not to mention his cultural significance.

The age of the Lakota hunter-warrior, which began countless generations ago, ended when our ancestors gave up the free-roaming, nomadic hunting life. The buffalo were gone, and living on reservations meant that facing their most persistent enemy—whites and their sense of Manifest Destiny—on the field of battle was no longer a viable option. A last resistance was, of course, at Wounded Knee in 1890, but thereafter the main enemies were uncertainty and white missionaries. When the ingrained sense of being the provider was supplanted by government annuities, an ancient and necessary societal role was no more.

Some men obviously contemplated what had happened and considered what could be done, but the overwhelming burden of sudden and traumatic change proved to be a formidable obstacle. No immediate answers were forthcoming to mitigate the dilemma, and the availability of liquor proved to be the final downfall for some Lakota men. It had to have been confusing, at the very least, for Lakota men at Camp Robinson. There was no more need to hunt, except perhaps for rabbits and other small game, and the very enemy whose defeat they had dedicated themselves to was now in control of their lives.

That's when the women stepped up.

While the overarching and crushing realities of no more buffalo to hunt and the authoritative presence of the whites were at least two of the specters faced constantly, starting in the 1860s, there were others. Life had to go on, and it had to be lived daily, and fortunately those challenges were not ignored by Lakota women.

During good times and bad, Lakota women were the focal point of family, they were the teachers, nurturers, and problem solvers. And at no time in recent history were they more critically needed than when the reservation era began. While some sons and husbands were lamenting that it would have been better to die in battle than to face a life of drudgery and boredom under the whites, their mothers and wives were doing what Lakota women had always done: they were taking care of their families. If they had not done that, during those first few years of agency/reservation life, and then in the subsequent generations, there would be—in my opinion—very little, if nothing, left of our culture.

Much has been written about Lakota history up to the reservation era, and to a certain extent after relocation to the "Great Sioux Reservation" in 1877. Not as much written information—good or bad—is available from 1900 to approximately 1950. Those were the decades that determined how we would transition into another culture and to what extent our own culture would be diminished. Obviously, there have been losses, but if not for the steadfastness of Lakota women, the losses would have been greater. Because they functioned as they always had, as the focal point of family and as the first teachers of children, they reduced the loss, they saved our culture. They did that by telling stories, speaking the language, and passing on family, community, and band history.

The pre-reservation Lakota hunter-warrior is no more. This does not mean, however, that out of the ashes of assimilation and cultural absorption, a new model of hunter-warrior, that necessary societal role, cannot arise. A new version that is based on the ancient traditions of protector and provider but that is also aware and attuned to the new forces, influences, problems, and enemies that threaten the Lakota family and culture today, up to and including alcohol, drugs, and domestic abuse. Then we, as Lakota men, might finally be able to measure up to the efforts and sacrifices made by our mothers and grandmothers in that time when we lost our way. Then, as our grandfathers and great-grandfathers did, we can once more take up the sacred duty of defending the helpless ones, armed and enabled by the ancient and strong values and habits they lived by, while at the same time informed, educated, and willing to face the here and now. In that way, though our grandfathers had to give up the gun and the horse, we can learn from that painful episode that often what is in the hand is not as strong as what is in our hearts and wills. After all, it was always the weapons powered by the will and the heart of the warrior that brought victory.

Then, and only then, will the Lakota hunter-warrior cease to be only yesterday's hero.

You Must Help Others Before You Think of Yourself

The Origins of Leadership

Not many of us in the course of everyday life give consistent thought to the subjects of leaders and leadership—except, of course, when election time rolls around and we are assailed by print ads and radio and television commercials. However we may feel about that assault on our senses and sensibilities, we should never forget that our lives have been and will always be affected by our elected politicians, from mayor to governor to president. Unless, of course, Turtle Island is returned to the original inhabitants who were doing quite well with all aspects of life, including leaders and leadership, until the invaders arrived from Europe. We can hope.

Because it is such an important aspect of our contemporary lives, leadership should be everyone's concern; we need to know how it does and does not work. There are obviously many approaches to leadership and many kinds of leaders. It would seem that most of the world has adopted the authoritarian approach, wherein power is vested in one position or office or one group. Words such as *monarchy, autocracy, democracy,* and *oligarchy* are used to describe how societies and nations are "governed" by concentrated interests. Every one of those systems has leaders, and those leaders work to perpetuate the system. And the primary and perpetual benefit is to the system rather than the people that enable the system by their labor or resources. When all is said and done, control is the underlying purpose of any system that purports to "govern." Control is wielded by one person with absolute power or by one group with absolute power. The power to control in a monarchy or autocracy is vested in one person, and in an oligarchy one group wields control. While a democracy outwardly appears to be government by the people whose wishes and opinions are articulated and acted on by elected representatives, we know that to be a facade. The representatives (legislators) that are to act on the people's wishes invariably set themselves up as the authority, or the base of power. In the American democracy, however, the real power rests with lobbyists—essentially corporate America—who control the legislators with money. Consequently, the United States of America is an oligarchy.

A monarch is a controller, not a leader. A dictator is a controller, not a leader. In any form of government there are people in positions of power who are elected, appointed, or who have simply taken control, and each and every one of those people labels themselves as "leaders." Anyone who has the power of broad and unlimited authority behind him or her, or the power of an armed force, or the power of a mindless mass of enablers, is a controller.

It can be argued that Hitler was a leader because he convinced an entire nation that fascism was their salvation. But it can also be argued that he convinced them by controlling what they heard, how they heard it, and how often they heard it. He was a controller, but history softens his sins by calling him the "leader" of Germany.

The word *leader* is part of our vocabulary, and how we define it is more than a matter of semantics. In the broadest of definitions, a leader is one who influences the actions and attitudes of others. Of course, that influence can be for bad or good. Even when we narrow the definition to "one who influences the actions and attitudes of others by example," it can still be for bad or good. Therefore, the role and the purpose of a *leader* is defined by what and who he or she leads. And, of course, a purpose or a mission is always part of the process.

The leader of a group is selected, supported, and followed because he or she represents and espouses the ideals and purpose of that group, be it the Saturday Sewing Circle, the Boy Scouts of America, the Republican Party, or the Ku Klux Klan. Some of us, or perhaps many, follow an idea or principle as much as we do an individual, but no matter what we follow, we empower that which we follow. A principle or a "leader" without followers is simply a failed idea or nothing more than a loud voice.

Lakota people had a unique and effective way of dealing with bad leaders: they simply stopped following them. It was told that a headman who had become too self-centered and arrogant awoke one morning to find that his family's lodge was the only one left in the village. The people had moved away during the night. This story is a word to the wise, a reminder that a leader's first responsibility is the people's welfare.

There are many forms of leadership and many ways to lead. One size does not fit all.

Pre-reservation Leadership

Authority is a concept that was not part of Lakota thinking before consistent contact with white people; it was not part of the functioning of a community or village. We now know the word and what it means in English and that the concept was and is an essential part of European and Euro-American society. Authority is certainly essential to tribal governments today, and we have inextricably entwined the word and the concept with another word—*leadership*. However, leadership in pre-reservation Lakota society had nothing to do with wielding authority. The fact that we think it did is another example of the influence of the colonizer.

Contemporary Lakota/English dictionaries list words for *authority* because the first whites to take a scholarly interest in Lakota and Dakota assumed that the concept existed in our culture. Instead of accepting that some Lakota and Dakota words and concepts did not exist in English, they took the "close enough" approach. For example, the Lakota word for "strength, power, and enablement" is *wowasake* (who-wah-sha`h-keh). White lexicographers in the late 1800s and early 1900s decided it was "close enough" to *authority* and listed it as such. The word *wowasake* was used in more than one context; it described physical strength, or power associated with nature such as lightning, wind, flood, and so on, or an act or thought enabled by agreement, permission, or social norms. For example, *Wowasake etan woglake* means "He spoke because he was enabled (by permission)." In other words, the group or community allowed or asked that person to speak for them. None of this usage states or even implies the English definition of *authority*.

Unfortunately, there are many other instances where white linguists and scholars took editorial license and made Lakota and Dakota words fit English meanings, concepts, and definitions. My father and I had a chuckle when we had the opportunity to talk about the movie *Dances with Wolves*. It is rife with historical and cultural inaccuracies and misrepresentations, beginning with the title translated in Lakota—*Sunkmanitu Tanka ob Waci*. The English title then should have been *Dances with the Big Dog Who Lives Where the People Do Not*. Imagine that emblazoned across a marquee, or hearing the title announced at the Academy Awards—and the Oscar goes to… Nowhere in the Lakota translation is the word for "wolf." *Sunka* is "dog," *manitu* is "away from people" or "where the people are not," *tanka* is "big" or "large," *ob* is "with," and *waci* is "to dance" or "dancing" or "dances." The correct word for "wolf" is *mayaca* (mah-yah-chah). It is likely derived from the habit of wolves to live in hillsides, deep gullies, or riverbanks—*maya*. In any case, the correct Lakota translation is *Mayaca ob Waci*. *Sunka manitu* refers to wolves, coyotes, and foxes as a group. The word for coyote is *mayasle* or *mayasleca*, and for fox it is *sunkagi*, *sungi*, or *tokala*.

There is not an overabundance of Lakota/English dictionaries, and while one or two of the more recent editions relied heavily on Lakota speakers, none of them apparently had editorial authority to ensure that only culturally correct definitions or usages were given. Languages do change, and more than a few of the indigenous languages still spoken today have been influenced by English. In my opinion, it is imperative that the pre-English (or other European) definitions and usages be given first, especially with definitions pertaining to *god* and *spirit*, since the Christian influence is usually prominently mentioned.

In any case, since the topic for this discussion is leadership, it will be necessary to throw into the mix words such as *government*, *leader*, *chief*, and the aforementioned *authority*, and how they did or did not fit into the pre-reservation model of Lakota leadership.

Most dictionaries have a few definitions of the word *government*:

- The governing body of a nation, state, or community,

- The system by which a nation, state, or community is governed, or

- The actions or manner of controlling or regulating a nation, organization, or people.

Any form of government has rules, regulations, codes, and laws in order to govern, and a system of enforcement and/or penalties and punishment when they are not followed. Pre-reservation Lakota societies—the villages/communities and larger bands—did not have any form of government. In other words, no one was tasked with the responsibility to see that people were acting in a generally acceptable manner, because it was not necessary. Proper conduct was largely established by societal norms and cultural values, and the immediate and extended family mitigated any misconduct. Family matriarchs and patriarchs were the finally arbiters.

To put it another way, Lakota communities/villages were self-governing within a society that valued free choice and individual freedom very highly. The concept and use of authority has no place in such a society, and yet there were individuals who rose to positions of leadership. Some of those individuals were leaders for decades and a few for a lifetime.

I enjoy looking at historic photographs of Lakota and Dakota people, some dating back as far as the 1870s. Most are of what I call the post-nomadic era, after our ancestors submitted to agency and reservation life. There are likely hundreds taken of the "Wild West" performers who traveled to Europe. One of those was of one of my great-grandfathers, a medicine man, who traveled to England and reportedly danced before Queen Victoria. Most photographs are of men in traditional garb, usually wearing a feather bonnet, or holding some type of weapon or a pipe. Some photographers had props on hand, such as a pipe or a "tomahawk," for subjects to hold as they posed standing or sitting.

One small detail I find interesting is that many, if not most, of the Lakota men in photographs are referred to as "Chief." Whether that is a designation given by the photographer or by the man himself is the question. Some of the men we know were leaders, such as Sitting Bull, Swift Bear, and Lone Horn.

And it is entirely possible that each and every man identified as a "chief" in a photograph was, indeed, a leader or a headman. Still, it brings to mind a popular axiom applied to a situation when too many people were telling too few what to do and how to do it—"Too many chiefs and not enough Indians."

Those photographs also bring to mind something that is at least annoying to me, if not troubling—the word *chief*. It was popularized in early dime novels and movies and implied and sometimes outright stated that "Chief Such-and-Such" was the guy who was in charge, the man who had the authority to tell other Indians what to do. A minor character in a recent Tom Selleck television western was a daughter of Red Cloud. Selleck's sidekick (the usual grizzled old white man who knew everything about Indians, of course) knew she was a chief's daughter because of the red stripe painted in the part of her hair. The implication was, naturally, that a daughter, or son, of a "chief" had a special status higher than that of other ordinary Indians. There was such a custom of painting the part of a woman's hair, but it had nothing to do with being the daughter of a "chief." (Two kinds of indigenous inhabitants are always misrepresented in movies: Natives and wolves.)

While these kinds of details are small within the broader and ugly history of white and Native interaction on this continent, the take-away by non-Native audiences is not small, and it is lasting. And when a knowledgeable Native person points out such historical or cultural mistakes, the usual rebuttal is "But I saw it in *Dances with Wolves*," or "I read it in such-and-such a book"—one written by a white author, of course.

The bottom line is the daughters of "chiefs" did not have special status, mainly because there were no "chiefs" (a bit anti-existentialist, perhaps, but true nonetheless). The title of "chief" is an annoying thorn in history because it was arbitrarily conferred upon Native men who were thought to be in charge. Lewis and Clark were among the first to do this where the Dakota and Lakota were concerned. And it has not stopped. An ethnocentric assumption was made by Lewis and Clark and others that, because authority was the foundation of governance and control in white society, it had to be the same among Native peoples. It was not.

There were leaders in Lakota and Dakota society, and leadership was a necessary component to the welfare of the people. Pre-reservation communities had leaders identified and known to the community as such, and such men were either *civilian* or *military* leaders, and they had a place within a loose hierarchy of leadership. That hierarchy was categorized as follows:

The Meeting or Gathering of Old Men

Medicine Men

Civilian Leaders/Headmen   Military Leaders

Warrior Societies   Experienced Men/Warriors

Younger Men/Warriors

The Gathering of Old Men

The "village council" was more commonly known as the Gathering of Old Men, and their group consisted of old men no longer consistently physically capable of taking the field as proficient fighting men. When a man's diminished skills became a liability and might put other men at risk in a combat situation, he refrained from participating in military activities. That is not to say these men were incapable of other activities. Many were hunters well into older age, even their late seventies. Hunting was physically challenging, but unless a man was physically debilitated, it was still a way to contribute to a family's needs. Furthermore, it required knowledge, patience, and marksmanship. Attributes that old men had in spades. And it was an opportunity to help hone the hunting skills of younger hunters, such as grandsons.

At this phase in life a man could take his place in the Gathering of Old Men. There, the knowledge he had gained from a lifetime of experience was the foundation for wisdom, and so he entered that final phase of his life. Many would argue that wisdom was just as important a contribution as anything else done on behalf of the community and nation, perhaps even more.

There are two important factors regarding the Gathering of Old Men. One, they had no authority to instruct or direct, and two, they were heavily influenced by the women in their families; therefore, though women were not physically present any time the old men gathered to talk and debate about issues, circumstances, or problems, each man took with him the thoughts and opinions of the women in his family. In that way, the influence of women was extremely significant.

Regarding the first factor, the function of the Gathering of Old Men was to debate and advise. For the purposes of this discussion, we can imagine that a village or community had twenty old men who made up that council, that gathering. Let us further imagine that the average age of those old men was seventy. Therefore, in that gathering would be fourteen hundred years of knowledge and experience, and that knowledge and experience would be brought to bear on any situation, circumstance, or problem brought before those old men. After exhaustive discussion and debate, and often argument, wise advice and opinion would be given.

That advice would be announced to the people in the community/village by the *Eyapaha* (eh-yah-pah-hah), meaning "he who announces," a trusted messenger with a powerful voice.

The messenger would report the conclusion or conclusions the Gathering of Old Men had reached. Nowhere in the message or announcement was any sort of direction, instruction, or a set or orders for the people to follow. It was simply the best advice the old men could give to address or mitigate the situation brought before them. Thereafter, it was entirely up to the people in the community to follow that advice, or not.

For this discussion I listed the hierarchy of leadership with the Gathering of Old Men at the top. In reality those old men in any pre-reservation community or village regarded themselves as being at the bottom, bearing the weight of responsibility for everyone else in the community.

Medicine Men

As mentioned previously, medicine men were healers and spiritual advisers. A community, depending on the population, might have a few medicine men, as was usually the case. Some of them might be part of the Gathering of Old Men, but as a separate group they were a significant influence on the old men. And individually and as a group, their insights, opinions, and advice were highly valued and frequently solicited.

Civilian Leaders (Headmen) and Military Leaders

There were several men in each community (which might comprise a few or several villages) who were designated, more or less, as headmen. Perhaps a more accurate way to describe them would be "leaders in reserve." These civilian leaders would be called on in any situation not associated with military activity, such as communal bison hunts, a village move, or a nonmilitary emergency. A few men might have a dual designation as civilian headmen and military leaders.

If anyone in the leadership hierarchy had any level of authority, by modern definition, it was civilian and military leaders when they were called up to solve a problem or take action. For the duration of the activity they had the ability to make decisions and issue orders.

In a given community the headmen, usually four, were selected by the council of old men, and they were known as the *Naca* (nah-chah). Selection was based primarily on experience and record of achievement. Each of the four then chose helpers or assistants, usually four per headman, to carry our assigned tasks—tasks that were for the express purpose of ensuring the safety of the community or helping and advising villagers/community members to do their part in the activity. Therefore, for example, in an event such as a village relocating, sixteen men—four for each headman—were responsible for carrying out tasks intended to conduct the move safely and efficiently. The four headmen observed and received reports from their helpers and made decisions to mitigate, reassess, and streamline efforts. Because the villagers understood that the headmen were acting in the best interest of their safety and well-being, they followed instructions and directives issued by the headmen through their helpers. When the new village site was reached, the lodges erected, and the move completed, the duties and responsibilities of the *Naca* and their helpers ended until the next time they were needed.

Warrior Societies and Experienced Older Men/Warriors

Prior to the move, the four headmen would select the members of a warrior society (and sometimes more than one society) to ride as guards, essentially the first line of defense to meet any threat. A relocation activity usually required more than a day, and during the night or nights, the warrior societies would stand watch as sentinels. Their duties ended when the move was completed. Warrior societies performed the same service when entire villages/communities moved for a communal bison hunt.

A warrior society was, if you will, a club for warriors, but it was far from simply having meetings to tell war stories. Throughout the band or nation there were several warrior societies, some more common than others. Some had larger memberships, and some had limited memberships and were more exclusive. The general purpose shared by all warrior societies was to educate young warriors regarding the duties and responsibilities of the war fighter, and to teach a particular philosophy or espouse a certain identity or purpose of a society. Each society reinforced the primary duty of the warrior, which was to defend the helpless ones.

In Lakota society, the calling of the war fighter or warrior was not to make war, but to confront the causes of conflict— hate, arrogance, mean-spiritedness, cruelty, mistreatment of helpless people, and so on. The overall commitment carried out by each warrior was and is summed up in the words of a traditional Lakota warriors honoring song: *Nipikin kta ca lecamuyelo,* which means, "I do this so the people will live." The act or commitment referred to by "this" meant anything up to and including giving his life in battle. These were the kinds of ideals and philosophies continually reinforced by warrior societies. Protecting their families, and especially the helpless ones, was the sacred duty, and giving their lives to that commitment was the highest honor achievable.

It was said Crazy Horse started a warrior's society after the death of his younger brother, and invited every man who had suffered the same kind of loss to join. One can assume that in the company of others who knew the same pain, there was some sense of comfort. As for all societies, there was a common bond.

In many cases, members wore certain symbols or colors. Many of them painted their faces the same way before going into battle or for social occasions, or painted their horses with the same symbols and patterns.

There were societies for which membership requirements were specific, such as the Red Feather Society. This one was made up of warriors who had been wounded in battle; its symbol was a feather painted red. Another society crossed tribal lines and was known by a few different names. Among the Lakota it was the *Tokala Wica*, or Kit Fox Society, and among the Cheyenne it was the Dog Soldiers. Membership was by invitation only. The Kit Foxes and Dog Soldiers society members were known for a particular ritual they often performed in battle, especially when the situation might seem hopeless. Each member carried a long, red, braided rope or a narrow sash, about twenty feet in length. In order to inspire and motivate other warriors and society members, a Kit Fox or Dog Soldier would stake an end of the rope or sash to the ground, and thus pledge to fight until victory was achieved or he was killed. The pledge would be fulfilled in only one of three ways: the stake could be pulled up by another society member, the battle was won, or the warrior was killed. The Kit Foxes and Dog Soldiers were admired and respected by their fellow warriors, and feared by anyone who faced them in battle.

Whatever philosophy, ritual, or markings set warrior societies apart from each other, the common theme for all of them was service and dedication to their families, community, and nation. And there was another important service warrior societies provided to the communities and the band and nation overall: they taught young men the value of leadership by example.

Not every warrior in a community joined a warrior society, but their commitment to the duty and responsibility of being a warrior was as strong as that of other men. The length of time a man was physically capable of taking to the field as a full-fledged fighting man was approximately thirty years, into the late forties. Assuming, of course, that he did not suffer a debilitating wound in battle, or a like injury while hunting, or was killed. It was not unusual for some men to be active warriors into their mid-fifties.

Lakota communities did not have a standing army whose only duty for a specified period of time was to be a war fighter. Boys were trained to fulfill the two necessary societal roles of provider and protector: the hunter and the warrior. Every man was both and functioned as the hunter more than he did as the warrior. Furthermore, only about 10 to 15 percent of a given community's population were active hunters and warriors. So, for example, a winter village of a hundred people would have ten to fifteen fighting men. When villages came to together from spring to late autumn, there were more warriors.

That group of older warriors, from the age of mid-thirties on, was a valuable source of experience. When it was time to select a *Naca*, the council of old men looked to this group of experienced men as much as they did to the warrior societies.

Whether a man was a member of a warrior society or not, he had learned from his teachers and mentors that leadership was a necessity for warriors when operating as a group. This was not an issue with scouts, however, because in most cases, a scout carried out his assignment alone. In the rare instances where there was more than one, leadership fell to the older and more experienced man, or it was simply a nonissue when two highly experienced men were in the field together.

Leadership status was not conferred. It was earned. Two factors always set a warrior apart from others: a solid record of achievement in the field, and common sense. And more often than not, a warrior who was known for both displayed two other important characteristics: selflessness and leading by example. Common sense and selflessness were often the factors that decided whether a battle was won or lost, and a man who consistently demonstrated both was a man to follow. No one, not the council of old men or the headman of a warrior society, could tell any warrior which leader to follow. That was a choice made by each fighting man.

The record of achievement and the character of any man who was considered a leader were known to the entire community. Therefore, a man could not misrepresent known facts, although some tried. Good men let their records and their actions speak for themselves. There were also many reluctant leaders throughout Lakota history, men who aspired to be good warriors but were reluctant to accept the status of leader. Crazy Horse, it is said, was one of those who did not want to be a leader.

To Lakota society in general, and certainly to those who were good leaders, leadership was not a prize or a path to fame. Leadership was a sacred calling. It was, to say the least, a weighty responsibility. The underlying responsibility of being a leader was that one gave up oneself and put others first.

In pre-reservation Lakota society, there was a tradition of identifying young men whom the community believed possessed the requisite *character* to be leaders. Usually, they were presented, as it were, every four years to the band or nation at large. As a group they were called *Wicawawoptecasni* (wee-chah-wah-woh-pteh-chah-shnee), meaning "men worthy of praise."

A feast was held, usually in the summer, and invitations were sent out far and wide. The presentation of the "men worthy of praise" was a significant social occasion because it was a display of a very important aspect of Lakota society. The families of each man selected—and there were usually four young men—or a quilling society of older women, made a special shirt for each young man. Each shirt was made from four tanned bighorn sheep hides; one hide for the front, one for the back, and one each for the sleeves. Each shirt was elaborately decorated with dyed porcupine quills, which were used before glass beads became a trade item, and each shirt represented or displayed something unique to each young man.

On the day of the feast the young men were seated in the middle of the village, with the people gathered around them. A respected elder, man or woman, was called upon to speak to them. That elder spoke words that were at the core of how leadership was regarded and defined in Lakota culture. A version is as follows:

> To wear the shirts you must be a man above all others. You must help others before you think of yourselves. Help the widows and those who have little to wear and to eat and have no one to speak for them.
>
> Do not look down on others or see those who look down on you, and do not let anger guide your mind or your heart.
>
> Be generous, be wise, and show fortitude so that the people can follow what you do, and then what you say.
>
> Above all, have courage and be the first to charge the enemy, for it is better to lay a warrior naked in death, than to be dressed well with a heart of water inside.

The young men who were given the shirts were known as "Shirt Men" or "Shirt Wearers." They were certainly expected to be leaders, but there was an expectation over and above that. *They were expected to live their lives beyond reproach as an example to everyone.* If the truth were told, not a single one of them, those who were thought to be "worthy of praise," fulfilled that expectation. It is important to understand, however, that the rationale behind that expectation was not for any or all of the Shirt Men to be perfect but rather to strive to be, and in doing so demonstrate that perfection is not as important as selfless service and good character.

The second lesson was just as important, that leadership is necessary in all walks of life. On a personal note, if there was one overall lesson we should take away from this all-but-forgotten aspect of pre-reservation Lakota society, especially for our contemporary leaders—Native or not—is that *leadership is a responsibility, not a prize.*

The Code of the Lakota Hunter/Warrior

There are countless images and descriptions of the Lakota male in art, movies and television, documentaries, nonfiction books, comic books, and novels. The overwhelming majority of the painting, filming, writing, and drawing was done by white males, whose research was based on the work of other white males. The overall result is a skewed representation of the real thing. There are a few works by white authors, artists, and documentarians that are accurate, but they are the exception rather than the rule. A positive change in recent years is that non-Native writers, artists, and filmmakers are approaching reliable Native resources to seek accurate historical and cultural information. It is frustrating, however, that the skewed image of the Lakota male remains embedded in white America's consciousness.

My insight into and knowledge of the Lakota male of the past comes from two sources. The first is the stories told by my grandparents and other Lakota people of that generation, and the second is from knowing my grandfather and other Lakota men of his generation.

The biggest blessing of my childhood was, without a doubt, being raised by my maternal grandparents. That time and that environment put me in contact with many Lakota people of their generation, and some who were older. And, obviously, all of them were valuable sources of information. They were walking, talking repositories of history and culture. More than a few of them, such as my grandfather, had been born before 1900. One of my grandmothers—and there were many—was born, she thought, around 1880, four years after the Greasy Grass Fight (Battle of the Little Bighorn). So that generation's parents were born around 1860, or before. Therefore, much of the information and many of the stories they heard were from the pre-reservation era, which means prior to 1860.

All the elders, all the grandmothers and grandfathers, told stories and imparted information. However, as a boy I heard from my grandfather and many other men the stories and information pertaining to men in Lakota society. My girl cousins heard stories and information from the grandmothers and other women about the role of women. That, in itself—women teaching girls and men teaching boys—was an ancient tradition, one still being honored in the late 1940s and early 1950s much more extensively than it is today. And it is because of that tradition that I know something about the societal role of the Lakota male, the role of the hunter/warrior.

As I've stated before in this book, during the pre-reservation era, the Lakota male had two broad societal roles and responsibilities: he was the provider for and protector of family and community. Within those broad roles, which every male fulfilled concurrently, were also the roles of son, husband, father, uncle, grandfather, teacher, horse trainer, bow-and-arrow maker, tracker, and sometimes traditional healer, among others.

The Making of the Hunter/Warrior

By the age of twelve it, was not uncommon for a Lakota boy to be self-sufficient as a hunter. He had the basic skills and knowledge to survive alone, away from other people, if it was necessary. By the time he was sixteen or seventeen, he had learned all the requisite skills to be a fighting man, having been trained, mentored, and tested by members of his own family as well as others. In the eyes of his family and the community/village, he was an adult because he was ready to contribute to the welfare of his family and the community. From that point on, it was a matter of gaining experience and constantly honing his skills and abilities. Up until about his mid-twenties, he was allowed to sit at the edge, the periphery, of the conversations of older men and elders. His sole responsibility was to listen, absorb, and learn. From his mid-twenties on, he was invited into the conversations and thus began to develop intellectually, and he began to form his own opinions and perspectives about all that was part of his continuing development as a man—perhaps by then being a father—and the calling of the hunter/warrior. And it was also at this juncture that he began to think more and more of the spiritual aspect of his life's journey, perhaps delving into the deeper meaning of awareness, selflessness, and sacrifice. Those three attributes were at the core of the code of the hunter/warrior.

When I was a boy my grandfather crafted a bow and four arrows for me, and taught me how to use them. (It was the only method I knew for many years until I began to read about European methods, and was surprised to learn there were other ways to shoot a bow, and that not all bows and arrows in the world are the same.) He was a very hands-on teacher and actively demonstrated each of the steps involved in the simple phrase "shooting a bow and arrow." These are steps he showed me:

- Stand with shoulders in line with the target;

- Simultaneously hold the bow at the handle in one hand (right for me), grab the arrow by the nock (the end with the fletching) with the other hand (left for me), and remove from the quiver;

- Nock or place the arrow on the bow string with the draw hand (left for me), making sure the arrow shaft is resting on the bow hand;

- Cant the bow or lean it slightly, in my case to the left, while focusing on the target (in this case it was a canvas ball stuffed with grass);

- Keeping eyes on target, begin to draw (pull back on the string), peripherally seeing the arrow in line with the center of the target;

- Continue drawing and do not stop, release.

My grandfather made everything look easy, but I learned it was a bit more complicated than it appeared. It does become easier with repetition—hours and hours of repetition.

I was amazed by his marksmanship. He consistently hit that canvas ball, which was probably six inches in diameter—consistently meaning eight out of ten times at a distance of approximately twenty-five yards, and sometimes farther. And every time we shot, he placed that ball at a different distance. In the beginning, my arrows at least flew in the general direction of the ball. After days and days of practice, I could place some of my arrows within a foot or two.

During one of our practice sessions (which were not daily since we had chores to do), he mentioned that the best marksmen in any village were the old men. Shooting a bow was something they had done regularly since they were five or six years old. When they were younger and stronger, their bows were powerful. As they grew older and began to lose arm-, shoulder-, chest-, and back-muscle strength, they usually shaved down the inside or back of the bow, thus making it easier to draw. But even into old age, men practiced with their bows in order to continue hunting and to use in battle, if necessary.

Later I learned that men practiced regularly with the weapons they used as hunters and fighting men. Out of an ash tree branch about an inch thick, my grandfather made what he called a "rabbit stick" for me. It was about eighteen inches long, with a slightly smaller branch protruding from the thicker end (it roughly resembled a capital *L*). He taught me how to throw it to make it spin in a flat circle. It was more than an adequate weapon for bringing down squirrels, cottontail rabbits, and sage hens up to a range of fifteen or twenty yards.

Mere proficiency with a hunter's weapon was not the objective of constant practice; every man strived for deadly skill. The weapons a hunter used were a longer hunting bow and a shorter buffalo bow. The buffalo bow was very powerful in order for its arrow, usually shot from horseback, to pierce the hide of a bison. The hunter also used a sling to throw egg-sized stones, the "rabbit stick," and a long buffalo lance, which was half again as long as a man was tall and sometimes twice over. Every man practiced consistently because the level of his skills, along with patience and his ability as a tracker, determined how well his family ate.

The weapons of a fighting man were a knife, a war club, a short bow, and a lance. The lance was only as long as a man was tall, and contrary to movies and novels, it was not a throwing weapon. The knife, the war club, and the lance were primarily for close combat, otherwise known as "hand-to-hand," either on foot or on horseback. One of the requisites for every village site, especially from spring to fall, was an area for men to practice. The area needed to be large enough to practice shooting a bow from a galloping horse. Sometimes the practice was part of the regimen for boys in training, and often the practice for older warriors was to face each other in simulated combat.

As with his hunter persona, the man as the war fighter strived for deadly skills, knowing that those skills could mean the difference between life and death for him, his fellow warriors, and the helpless ones.

My grandfather, like many of his generation, had a habit of revealing a skill or a bit of knowledge when it suited him, or likely when he felt I was ready. There was one instance, however, that seemed to be unplanned. One day he saw a long and nearly perfectly straight branch on an ash tree, over an inch in diameter. He cut the branch and trimmed it to match his height. Then, without comment or preamble, he began to make thrusts front and back, and otherwise spin and twirl that green pole. When he saw me watching (probably with my mouth hanging open) he told me that the routine he did was one that Lakota warriors used in battle in close quarters fighting with an enemy with a war lance. Years later I saw a striking similarity to a *kata*, a training exercise performed by a karate master to simulate fighting moves.

My grandfather bemoaned the fact that much specific and detailed knowledge about what he essentially described as a culture within a culture (the characterization is mine and not his), that of the Lakota hunter/warrior, had disappeared. It was in 1954, if memory serves, that he first demonstrated the practice routine with the war lance. By then, only a very few Lakota men still knew about the routine or how to do it. It is anyone's guess as to how many know about it today, and much less can demonstrate it. Perhaps a greater loss is the knowledge that the Lakota warrior was intensely committed to sacred calling.

Awareness was another extremely vital skill that the Lakota hunter/warrior constantly strived to improve. It was just as important as any weapon he carried in his hands.

Much is made about "spirit animals" in Native cultures, usually postulations from non-Native "experts" who still see Native peoples through a strange lens that shows us as "noble savages," as tree huggers that regularly commune with animals on some level. Remove the lens and you may realize that our ancestors were indeed in tune with nature, but this was because they were part of an environment they knew intimately and realistically. They had an honest awareness of how to survive in and with the natural environment. I can understand, though, how that level of awareness regarding the natural world could seem mysterious to people who came to this continent fearing it mightily.

Learning from the Wolf

One of the beings that early Europeans feared more than the devil itself was the wolf, and it's likely that some still do. They brought with them old fears, with stories of werewolves waiting in the dark to eat them or tear them limb from limb. Based on such fears, Europeans labeled wolves as *wanton killers* and described them as living and running in *packs*. That fear prompted them, for three hundred years, to shoot wolves on sight, and in the late 1800s and early 1900s, the US government hired hunters to trap and hunt them out of existence. The efforts were so successful that wolves were nearly extirpated below the 48th parallel, with only a few survivors on Isle Royale in Michigan. The fear-based myth about wolves was still real enough for the anti-wolf community—ranchers, farmers, hunters, and big game guides—to rabidly oppose the reintroduction of wolves into Yellowstone National Park. In spite of that, a few wolves were released into the park in the mid-1990s, and their impact, and that of their descendants, on the Yellowstone ecosystem has been positive. The opposition to wolves has not waned, and deregulation by the Trump administration will likely result in wolves once again being hunted and killed.

Yet, many indigenous cultures coexisted peacefully with wolves for thousands of years before the arrival of Europeans, the Lakota among them. Wolves were not a threat to people; in fact, wolves in the wild go out of their way to avoid contact with humans. And as Native societies observed the behavior of wolves, they learned basic facts about them. Wolves are a family unit, led by a mated pair, and in many cases (according to some ancient Native observers), the leader of the family, or the alpha wolf, was often the female. And the members of the group were generations of their children, with an occasional outsider adopted into the family.

Two characteristics the wolf possessed struck a chord with many Native people: it was a persistent hunter and it was always in tune with its environment. The prowess of the wolf as a hunter is attributed primarily to its physical attributes, such as keen sense of smell, sight, and hearing, not to mention that it was a long distance runner and had powerful jaws and sharp teeth. But while those attributes were impressive, they were not useful without the one virtue—as Native people saw it—that made them superb hunters. In spite of those marvelous physical attributes, wolf hunters failed many times before they succeeded. In spite of that, they persisted. Wolves knew how to persevere.

Native hunters, the Lakota among them, emulated the wolf. There was no way to acquire the wolf's physical attributes, of course, but perseverance was something they could learn. The wolf taught them that failure was not a deterrent.

Native people who closely observed the wolf could not measure how keen or sharp a wolf's senses were. They saw, however, that as wolves moved and traveled in their territories, they frequently paused to observe with their eyes, sniff the air with their noses, and listen intently with their ears. Native observers surmised that those immeasurably keen senses enabled the wolf to gather information, and to track and prey on animals such as deer and elk. Its nose could sense that an elk, for example, had passed through a part of the forest. Its ears could detect the slightest noise from great distances, and its eyes could see the slightest movement. In other words, a wolf knew what was happening in its immediate environment. That level of awareness could warn of danger or reveal how far away a deer or a herd of elk was.

The attribute of awareness was taught to young Lakota boys as a physical tool as well as a social and intellectual one. A Lakota man's role as a hunter and a warrior was connected to all aspects of his life. Not only did his actions and words have an impact on others, the reverse was true as well. And because a community was made up of individuals with all manner of opinions, preferences, tendencies, weaknesses, and strengths, all of which influenced actions, it was wise to be aware, as much as possible, of those factors as well.

The level of awareness depended on the extent to which anyone was willing to learn, and that resulted in the accumulation of knowledge. The pursuit of knowledge, the elders taught, was just as necessary to a people's survival as food, shelter, clothing, and security. Knowledge was a way to solve problems; it was a way for a society to thrive and develop.

But knowledge is also a stepping stone, an intellectual mechanism, if you will, that leads some to contemplate, to ponder. To contemplate, ergo to become a thinker, was the last phase of the journey to become *wica* (wee-chah), meaning "man," or to put it another way, "the complete man."

The word *wicasa* (wee-chah-shah) means "man," and it can and does mean everything from the basic gender label to the fulfillment of all that it meant to be a man in Lakota society—responsible, strong, defender, and so on.

Wica has two connotations. It was often used as the word for "warrior," and often with the word *zuya* (zoo-yah), which means "war" or "battle." A *zuya wica* is literally "war man," meaning "the man who is going to war or into battle." *Zuya wicasa* means the same; however, *wica* is on a higher level in that the man has accomplished more and is multidimensional—the kind of man referred to in Western culture as a "renaissance man." Some *wica* who seemed to be reaching higher or even rising above the physical world were thought to be mystics. They were the thinkers because they pondered, contemplating life, spirituality, and so on. They were often the kind of thinkers who sought the ultimate truth about whatever reality was. Crazy Horse, it is said, was such a man.

Just as a man endeavored to increase his skill with the bow and arrow even into his elder years, he also sought to develop an awareness of all the realms he knew existed in the physical and spiritual worlds. That was the fruition of being *wica*—the complete man.

As has been discussed, the journey of the hunter/warrior began at about the age of five or six. The first steps were basic and elemental, very much having to do with physical development and physical skill sets. A boy's teachers and mentors ensured that the requisite skills were developed beyond the point of basic proficiency. Along the way, each boy learned that although he embodied both personas—hunter and warrior—they were different. One provided for life and one protected life.

Contrary to what some might think or believe, the hunter/warrior did not want a glorious death. If anything he wanted a meaningful death, one that was part of an effort to protect the helpless ones or to win the day. What he preferred was to grow old with the love of his life, enjoy his grandchildren, and reach the status of elder knowing he had accomplished enough to have learned something in his life, and then take his place as an elder.

On Authenticity

In the late summer of 1952, when I was seven, lightning struck on the western slopes of the *Makizita Wakpa* (Misty or Smoky River) valley, now called the Little White, a few miles west of our house. Although it was not quite four miles away, we felt the ground shake, and I heard the air buzz with electricity several moments before the thunder blasted through the sky. *Wakangli* (wah-khan-glee) *na wakinyan* (wah-ghin-yanh), lightning and thunder, were a common occurrence on the northern plains in summer. Nevertheless, there were a few instances when they seemed so close I expected to see the flashing yellow eyes of the *Wakinyan*, the Thunder Beings.

Wakinyan Hotunpi (hoh-thun-bee) was the descriptor for thunder, and it meant literally "the Thunder Beings used their voices. *Wakangli* was colloquially "lightning," but it literally meant "they returned in a sacred/powerful manner."

My grandparents and I were awestruck by the bright and powerful show put on by the Thunder Beings that afternoon, and we were thankful for the rain that followed because it saved us from the watering the garden, at least for that day. The next morning my grandfather announced to my grandmother that he and I were going for a walk. We struck out west, taking an old familiar trail to the river. Crossing the stream turned milky brown by the rain, we kept heading west. A mile or so farther (and that estimate is given in this current moment because I did not know or care what a mile was at the age of seven),

I figured out where we were going. My grandfather wanted to find the spot where lightning had struck, and we did. Just below the top of a long, sloping ridge was a nearly perfect circle of scorched ground at least thirty yards in diameter. My grandfather surmised that it was raining when the lightning struck and that had prevented a grass fire. I recall that he was somewhat disappointed, and I knew why. He was hoping that the lightning had struck one of the ash trees on that slope. It clearly had not.

My grandfather was hoping for a lightning-struck ash tree because he wanted, at least once in his life, to make a *wakangli itazipa*—a "lightning bow."

Normally, once cut, an ash limb must be air dried and cured for at least three years for it to harden properly and be made into a bow. But one struck by lightning is dried and cured in a millisecond—provided the tree did not explode into hundreds of pieces. If a piece of the proper size is found from a lightning-struck tree, it can be crafted into an exceedingly strong and durable bow. A lightning bow, it was said, could cast arrows farther and faster than any other bow, because it was imbued with the awesome power of lightning.

This was truth, not myth, because more than one Lakota bow maker in the past had made a bow from a lightning-struck tree. My grandfather had looked since his teenage years for such a tree; he lived for eighty-eight years and did not find one.

Bows and arrows were important to my grandfather because they were part of his heritage, both culturally and individually. Seventy-seven years before lightning struck that slope above the *Makizita Wakpa*, his father (my great-grandfather) had gone into battle against the Long Knives at the Greasy Grass with an ash bow in his hand and a quiver filled with nearly thirty arrows. That battle occurred at the Little Bighorn River in Montana in 1876, and my grandfather was born in 1888.

My grandfather was a bow maker, and he crafted bows in the way he was taught, primarily by an uncle named Fast Hawk. My great-grandfather, the warrior of Greasy Grass, had died of Spanish influenza in 1896. Every bow my grandfather ever made in his life was made according to how he had been taught. He followed every step and used the same materials as his father and uncles did. Therefore, every bow he made was an authentic Lakota bow (the same for arrows).

Anything authentic is of undisputed origins. Therefore, because I make bows using the same methods my grandfather taught me, that his uncle taught him, that his father and grandfather taught him, my bows are authentically Lakota. And there is one final factor that authenticates the authenticity—I am Lakota. My grandfather said that only a Lakota can make a Lakota bow. So, as far as Lakota bows are concerned, that implies two primary factors that make them authentic: the design of the bow and the ethnicity of the bow maker. But there is a third factor, and that is materials. Lakota bows were made from hardwoods, mainly ash, oak, and chokecherry shrubs. Ash was used most often because of availability; there were more ash trees of the proper length and width than there were oak trees. There were even fewer chokecherry shrub stalks that were the height of a man and as thick as a man's forearm. In my opinion, based on experience, oak makes a better bow than ash.

Therefore, an authentic Lakota bow would be one made from ash, oak, or chokecherry wood using ancient Lakota designs, according to customary length and width; with a string made from the hamstring sinew of bison, elk, deer, or antelope; and crafted by a Lakota bow maker. That would mean that the only difference between such a bow made in 2019 and one made in 1819 would be two hundred years.

The same statement can apply to arrows. Arrow shafts were peeled hardwood and softwood stalks, cut to an approximate length no more than twenty-six inches, more or less. (Measurements for bows were based on the height of the archer and arrows on the length of the archer's arm and hand.) Other materials used to make arrows were feathers, sinew, and a stone point, usually chert (flint) and sometimes obsidian. Again, arrows were made according to a basic design using ancient crafting methods.

However, a certain material not available naturally in Lakota territories came along initially in about the 1840 to 1850 period and was quickly adapted for use on Lakota arrows and lances—iron. This was about the same time that glass beads appeared on the northern plains.

Lakota bow-and-arrow makers quickly found a certain type of iron very suitable for arrowheads, barrel hoop iron—the metal band or strap used to hold oaken barrels together. Those hoops or straps were thin and strong and could be cut with a cold chisel or melted down easily. They were the perfect material for arrowheads, and they were much more durable.

Similarly, the iron rims that encircled wagon wheels were just as suitable for the points on buffalo and war lances.

So in less than a generation, Lakota arrow makers switched from stone points to iron arrowheads. That change leads us to an interesting question: Because a material foreign to the Lakota was adapted to the crafting of arrows, did that render the arrow inauthentic?

Nothing else about the arrow changed—only the stone point discarded in favor of the iron point. All other materials and crafting methods remained the same, although arrow makers had to learn to work with iron.

There were two kinds of arrows: hunting and war. The hunting arrow was heavier and longer and had three feathers in its fletching. The war arrow was shorter and lighter and was fletched with two feathers. The back end of a stone hunting point had rounded shoulders, while the back ends of a war point were pointed or barbed. The same designs were incorporated into iron hunting and war points.

A Lakota hunting arrow with a stone point placed next to one with an iron point, made by the same craftsman, would be the same, with one exception: the points. Is the one with the iron point less authentic than the other?

An argument can be made that the arrow with the iron point is not authentic because of the use of a foreign material. Likewise, an argument can be made that authenticity is based more on crafting methods and design. Then, of course, we can begin making distinctions, such as pre- and post-iron. A Lakota arrow made with all-natural materials adhering to ancient designs is pre-iron and historically authentic. A Lakota arrow made with all natural materials, except the iron point, and adhering to ancient design is post-iron and also historically accurate. However, if we allow those distinctions are we obfuscating the very definition of *authentic*? Or, in a broader context, can we say that any arrow, now or then, made by a Lakota craftsman is a Lakota arrow?

I have a Lakota hunting bow that I made using the design and configuration my grandfather taught me, but the wood is hickory. There is not much hickory that grows on the northern plains, but it did in the lake country of northern Minnesota, where my Lakota ancestors once lived. Furthermore, the string is not natural sinew, it is synthetic, and finally, the hand tools I used—axes, splitting awls, drawknives, and files—are all modern tools. Do all these factors render my bow inauthentic? I have also made bows from Osage orange, a tree not indigenous to Lakota territory. But the bow is of Lakota design. Is that bow authentic? The issue goes on and on. I have made arrows of willow stalks, and I used the ancient crafting methods—some have stone points and others have iron points. I have made arrows out of commercially manufactured shafts of Sitka spruce and Port

Orford cedar, and I used natural feathers, and some have stone points and others have iron points. Are any or all of those arrows authentic? They all appear to be authentic.

My point is, while a definition of *authentic* is fairly simple and straightforward—"of undisputed origin"—how we perceive it is open to interpretation. But thus far this discussion has centered on artifacts, bows, and arrows. What happens to our perception of *authentic* when we begin to talk about language, beliefs, rituals, customs and traditions, or identity?

The incorporation of iron points onto arrows and lances and knife blades, among other objects, was, of course, a consequence of the westward encroachment of white people— Europeans and Euro-Americans. Obviously that encroachment forced itself into more than territory and did much more than alter weapons and tools and clothing and shelter. It affected the foundations of Lakota culture.

In the early 1840s, the great migration of white people from Missouri to California and Oregon was in its infancy. It followed a trail through the southern part of Lakota territory, and every summer hundreds of canvas-topped wagons rolled steadily east to west.

Astonishment, confusion, curiosity, disdain, and fear were likely some of the emotions Lakota people experienced as they witnessed the strange phenomenon. There was, of course, the hope that these immigrants and strangers were only passing through. But thousands of white people every summer for twenty years portended nothing good, and for certain they were the object of much debate and discussion, and more than a little prayer. Those debates and discussions were in Lakota, and any prayers said were also in Lakota. Today, when we Lakota talk about that same phenomenon of the Oregon Trail and the consequences it has wrought, we do so in English. Ironically, that is one of the consequences.

In the ensuing decades since that twenty-year event, and possibly because of it, have we as Lakota people lost our cultural authenticity? Perhaps a better question is: Have we lost touch with our origins?

The last question came to mind when, at one o'clock in the morning, I heard a rap concert blasting though the night at the Dakota Access Pipeline protest encampment along the Cannonball River. It was loud and intrusive and impossible to ignore. It comes to mind when I see tribal elders dressed in traditional garb and hear them utter Christian prayers at a gathering of several tribes, or when I hear Christian hymns sung in a Native language. It comes to mind when I hear elected tribal officials say the past is the past and we should move on, or when I watch them speak and behave exactly like white politicians. That question comes to mind when I see and hear young Native people disrespecting elders.

There are definite indicators that Native peoples, we Lakota included, have lost touch with our roots, our origins. We have lost touch with the values that were at the core of our identity. Too many of us think of ourselves as "Native Americans."

America as the melting pot has not worked for people of color. We brown-skins were already here living our dream, while Black people were brought here and dropped into a nightmare (to put it mildly), and it was no less traumatic for the Chinese and other Asians. Homogeneous America is a failed experiment because there is a white fear of racial and ethnic diversity. To white America, any person not white-skinned was "less than" or "not quite as good as." And it was that same white America that implemented the effort and policy to "kill the Indian and save the man" by stripping away our identity, our authenticity, as Native peoples. And when they did strip most of it away—or all of it in some cases—they still saw only the brown skin on the outside. The fact that we spoke their language and worshipped their god mattered not at all, and neither did the fact that some of us achieved success by being athletes, doctors, ballerinas, soldiers, and politicians. It mattered not because no matter how much we were like white people, we were not white. Worst of all, it mattered not to them that they decimated individual and cultural identity and damaged our authenticity.

That reality is evident when Native people are easily drawn to and become part of a different culture, a cult, a belief (religion), a philosophy, or a discipline. My heart sinks, and sometimes it breaks, when I see Native young people with dyed blond hair, or wearing gang colors and paraphernalia, backward baseball caps, nose rings, or baggy trousers, because I wonder if they feel that their Native identity and appearance is inferior. Or perhaps they think, or believe, that clothes, hair color, or nose rings are more relevant. I have learned something about Asian martial arts, but that does not make me Japanese or Korean (nor have I felt inclined to be "adopted" into an Asian culture).

I have always known who I am, that I am Lakota, and that that reality made me different from white people. And as I grew older I learned—as my grandparents had warned me—that as a Lakota person I was regarded as inferior. My grandparents had also said that was not true.

I still recall a simple lesson my grandmother taught me as a boy. Someone in my third grade class had called me "a dirty Indian," and I was hurt. After I told her, she took me out into the yard (by then we lived in town) and had me find a long, dried twig. She pointed to it and told me to call it a snake. I hesitated, of course, but she insisted. Feeling a bit silly I looked down at the twig and said (in Lakota), "You are a snake." She told me to watch the stick closely, and then asked me what it was. "Just a stick," I told her. "Did calling it a snake make it a snake?" she asked. Of course, it had not.

Over the years I learned other realities. I was just as smart as white students, and sometimes smarter. I could run just as fast, and sometimes faster. And because of the manners and the values I learned from my grandparents, I cared about white kids as people more than they cared about me in the same way.

On the one hand, a sense of identity and authenticity go hand in hand, and they can be a source of strength to enable one to face life's trials and tribulations, especially for anyone who lacks the advantages others might have. On the other hand, it can foster a sense of privilege if money is not an issue.

No one chooses to be born into a particular family or race or social status. That is pure chance. No one is born feeling inferior or powerless, neither is anyone born feeling superior or privileged. Those ideas are taught. Attitudes of superiority and privilege are taught by those who feel they can claim them. They in turn teach those who are different from them to feel inferior and powerless.

There are, sadly, ways to make anyone, or any group, feel inferior, and the use of labels is one. Words and phrases such as *minority*, *underprivileged*, *low income*, *uneducated*, *dropout*, *welfare recipient*, and so on. But sometimes a white person's assertion, intended or not, of white privilege, without a direct reference to other races, can be just as denigrating.

I recall hearing a college classmate announce his birthday one day, before the instructor arrived, by saying, "I'm free, white, and twenty-one!" He was voicing the axiom that separated him from everyone in the room who was not white, and there were at least three: two Japanese students and me. I sincerely doubt that it was anything more than naive youthful exuberance and not intended to denigrate anyone, but it could have had that effect.

My reaction to the statement was not so much a feeling of inferiority as a person; rather, I was reminded of the advantages I did not have. Being white gave my classmate a better chance for an education, getting a bank loan, renting a house, and timely service in a restaurant. Those advantages were an obvious part of his authenticity as a white person in the United States. To a certain extent, however, I did feel powerless because I could do nothing to change that reality. The only choice open to me was to adjust to those realities, and that meant realizing that being turned down for a bank loan was not so much a statement of creditworthiness as it was a judgment based on my brown skin. And I, as a brown-skinned person, had to keep that awareness in the forefront of my thinking in any and all situations and interactions with white people.

I worked hard at not feeling inferior, and most of that effort was to constantly remind myself that as an individual I was just as capable as any other person. Dealing with others judging me as inferior had nothing to do with my rights as a person, because in the minds of some white people, those rights were less or nonexistent because I was Lakota. Therefore, my sense of being equal to others was based entirely on my capabilities measured against or compared to theirs. As a seventh grader, a small town cop told me in no uncertain terms that in the eyes of the law, "You ain't nothing, 'cause white folks say what rights you got and what you don't got." So while, for the most part, I did not feel inferior as a person, I knew that I was at a disadvantage. That piece of "advice" from that cop comes to mind anytime I have to interact with a police officer of any kind, anywhere.

Thus while I am over twenty-one years of age, I am definitely brown and not white, so perhaps the only common ground I have with my former classmate is to be free—but not from white privilege or racism, and I am guessing that while he likely exercised one, he has never felt the sting of the other.

That was his authenticity as a white American, and mine, as a Lakota with a heritage of adaptability, was to let the wind blow through me. That has been one of our survival mechanisms to endure whatever is thrown at us.

The origins of the Lakota people, our society, and our culture is older than the word *Lakota*. Our ancestors developed a cohesive society and evolved because they accepted the realities of the natural environment and adapted to fit in. Our values, customs, traditions, and spiritual beliefs are based on our relationship and interaction with the Earth. Those are our origins. All of the aforementioned components of our culture enabled us to thrive as a society and exist without harming the natural environment, guided our interactions with other Native societies, and helped us deal with change—such as our ancestors' migration from the northern woodlands to the northern plains. External influences did not significantly alter our values, customs, traditions, or beliefs, and in some instances new things were incorporated. However, none of the circumstances that our ancestors faced and dealt with was as invasive and as persistent and as harmful as the interaction with white people. The words attributed to an old Lakota fighting man aptly and tragically characterized it: "I would rather fight a bear than face the treachery of the whites."

As a matter of fact, we Lakota are still adjusting to the impact of the whites, and among many adverse consequences is the loss of our true identity, which is to say we have lost the connection to our authenticity.

There was a time when Lakota children and young people literally pestered grandmothers and grandfathers for stories, much the same way today's generations ask for the latest version of Xbox or to see the latest superhero movie. I was one of those who constantly asked my grandparents to tell me stories. The difference between the stories I heard in the 1950s and the video games—and movies and television shows—Lakota children are playing and watching today is alarming: the stories connected me over and over again to my authentic heritage, while the video games, movies, and television shows are teaching my grandchildren's generation violence and white culture. In essence they are being desensitized to violence while learning a superficial culture. Perhaps that is the new heritage.

Each Lakota generation since that first one forced into boarding schools has experienced alienation from its culture and history. Strangely enough, the advent of movies created an unwitting accomplice that pulled Lakota people farther and farther away from the traditional influences and mechanisms that once taught them their heritage. As a grandparent with stories to tell, the competition for my grandchildren's time and attention is formidable, and it is loud, fast, glitzy, and in my face. While I am not opposed to children being entertained, I am opposed to the kind of entertainment that is currently available. It obscures and invalidates their heritage and cultural authenticity. This is an issue for today's Lakota parents and grandparents to face and mitigate because of the social and psychological impact on their children and grandchildren. Furthermore, we must face the fact that video games and other forms of visual entertainment are formidable obstacles to revitalizing our culture.

In the old days, there were no such distractions—at least none so powerful and invasive. By the late 1800s, however, the consistent presence of white people and Lakota children being shipped off to boarding schools was the beginning of the outright assault on and mission to eliminate our culture. (Hundreds of other tribes were experiencing the same agonizing dilemma.) The efforts by the parochial and government boarding schools were of course immeasurably more traumatic for Native children than are video games, television, and movies, but the consequence is still the same. The policy of separating and isolating children and forbidding them to speak their Native language, generation after generation, resulted in the loss of Native language skills and a disconnect from culture and history. And to put it bluntly, the distractions enabled by today's technology are finishing the task. It would seem, then, that Lakota language and culture are on their way to their ultimate demise aided by joysticks, superhero movies, and the glassy-eyed hypnosis of Lakota children. The sad reality is that we, adults and children alike, no longer live and breathe being Lakota. We put on regalia and dance at pow-wows for a few days out of the year, or perhaps we participate in traditional ceremonies, or something else "mostly Lakota" when we have the time in our busy lives, but for the most part our days are mainly filled with things not part of Lakota culture.

We are part of the mainstream culture in many ways. Our daily routines and behavior are, for the most part, like those of every other American citizen. Our children and grandchildren go to school, and if we have a job we go to work. We stress over rent, house and car payments, and myriad other bills, as well as health and family issues.

On a broader scale, we are construction workers, electricians, teachers, day laborers, carpenters, ranchers, law enforcement officers, nurses, janitors, social workers, musicians, bookkeepers, small business owners, politicians, doctors, clerical workers, and so on.

Perhaps the specific efforts of the government and churches to assimilate Natives into mainstream culture has waned somewhat, but that is due in part to the fact that we Natives are aiding assimilation by voluntarily acculturating to mainstream society. In a very real sense that is positive, but it comes at a price. As brown-skinned participants in mainstream society, many of us are disconnected from our Native cultures. That disconnect varies individually, of course, depending to what extent we were culturally influenced by our Native parents and grandparents.

In many Lakota communities today, there are still individuals and families who are more connected to traditional Lakota culture than most. During my childhood (six decades ago), however, nearly all of my grandparents' relatives and friends were staunchly traditional. Lakota was still spoken widely, though many knew English, and the interaction between and among Lakota people was—according to my grandparents—strongly reminiscent of the pre-reservation era. I recall summer gatherings under the auspices of the Episcopal Church, known as convocations, that I attended with my grandparents. Hundreds of Lakota people from every reservation in South Dakota attended and camped together for days. My fondest memory of those gatherings is of the way people greeted each other and talked to one another, with utmost courtesy, especially among the elders. And all conversations were in Lakota—except of course when someone spoke to a white priest, or any other white person there. All of my grandparents always mentioned that, although everyone was a member of the Episcopal Church, the cultural reality of being Lakota was still very strong in the 1940s and 1950s. Except for the reason behind having these Episcopal convocations and the white people there, many elders said it was like turning back time and being part of a village in the old days.

Since the 1860s, we have gradually lost that connection to our culture because white society and lifestyle have seduced us. Whether that was the intention of the framers of the policies of forced assimilation or not, it is now a sad reality. We have given in to and practice two of the most horrendous aspects of white society: materialism and lack of respect for our elders. The situation is further compounded by the fact that the younger Lakota generations did not hear the heartfelt and impassioned stories my grandparents' generations told—stories that were told with pride, exuberance, laughter, fondness, and often profound sadness. Therefore, we have lost connection to the reality that our culture was immeasurably better than the one we were forced into.

The heartless and tragic part of this process that we overlook as Native people is that white people were not encouraging, nor did they welcome us into their way of life; they were forcing us to transform before we could be accepted. A simple analogy is that whenever we welcome anyone into our homes, we allow that person to enter our home as who they are. We do not tell them to change their name, their clothes, their religion, or their politics before they enter. White people were, and still are, doing exactly that. *Kill the Indian and save the man,* though not a hollow mantra, is an outright lie. They certainly did everything to "kill the Indian," but they do not care about us as humans.

It does not matter to white society that we Lakota, and other indigenous peoples, have changed in order to enter. It does not matter how well we speak English, or that many of us have forsaken traditional beliefs to be Episcopalian or Catholic or members of the Masonic Temple. It does not matter that some of us have achieved the same pinnacle of success in the culture of materialism as they have. All that matters is the color of our skin. If this were not true, there would be no labels such as "Native American," "African American," "Asian American," or "Native American actor," "Native American writer," or "Native American doctor." The most telling factor is the absence of the label "white American" or "Euro-American." White people don't use these labels to describe themselves because they perceive themselves as the norm. But the fact is, they're just another factor in the reality of diversity, both in this country and around the globe.

For me, personally, nothing highlights that attitude of superiority and white privilege more than the story of Standing Bear and a small group of Ponca people he led back north from Indian Territory in 1879. The situation in Indian Territory was hand-to-mouth, one that brought illness and death for the different tribal groups there, and on January 2, 1879, Standing Bear and twenty-eight other Ponca fled north. After more than two months of walking, they found refuge among the Omaha people on their reservation. Weeks later, the Ponca were arrested and taken to Fort Omaha in eastern Nebraska, facing the real prospect of being returned to Indian Territory. A local newspaper editor, Thomas Tibbles, heard of their situation and enlisted the aid of two local lawyers, who petitioned the local court on behalf of Standing Bear and his small band. It became known as *Standing Bear v. Crook* because General George Crook was charged with the task of returning the Ponca to Indian Territory.

From the beginning it is apparent, at least to me, that expatriation, or the Ponca group's renunciation, in essence, of their own culture and nationality, was a critical factor in the case. Part of the initial petition read, in part:

[The Ponca] have made great advancements in civilization, and at the time of the arrest and imprisonment of your complainants, some of them were actually engaged in agriculture, and others were making preparations for immediate agricultural labors, and were supporting themselves by their own labors, and no one of these complainants, was receiving or asking support of the government of the United States.

The "great advancements in civilization" pointedly mentioned is, no doubt, the fact that the Ponca were in the process of planting crops when the army arrested them on the Omaha reservation. As far as I have been able to determine, this was not a "great advancement" at all because the Ponca were already an agrarian people, having lived along rivers and planting crops on bottomlands.

Standing Bear's case went to trial in April of 1879 and lasted two days. Nearly two weeks later, Judge Elmer Dundy issued an opinion, based largely if not entirely on Standing Bear's willing expatriation from his Ponca roots. Excerpts from the ruling are as follows:

> On the one side we have a few of the remnants of a once numerous and powerful, but now weak and insignificant, unlettered, and generally despised race. On the other, we have the representatives of one of the most powerful, most enlightened, most christianized nations of modern times. On the one side we have the representatives of this wasted race coming into this national tribunal of ours asking for justice and liberty to enable them to adopt our boasted civilization and to pursue the arts of peace, which have made us great and happy as a nation.

> The petition alleges in substance that the relators are Indians who have formerly belonged to the Ponca Tribe ... now located in Indian Territory; that they had some time previously withdrawn from the tribe and completely severed their tribal relations therewith, and had adopted the general habits of the whites, and were then endeavoring to maintain themselves by their own exertions.

> He also states that he informed that their ... final purpose to leave, never to return, and that he and his followers had finally, fully, and forever severed his and their connection with the Ponca Tribe of Indians, and to cut loose from the government, go to work, become self-sustaining, and adopt the habits and customs of a higher civilization.

There are many facets to the story beyond the legal aspects, and it does end well, though it must be said that Standing Bear and his twenty-eight relatives and friends endured extreme hardships for several long months. Standing Bear's son had died in Indian Territory of a white man's disease and had asked his father to take his body home. Standing Bear fulfilled his promise to do so, and the annals of history have few impassioned words that equal his statement to Judge Dundy:

> That hand is not the same color as yours, but if I prick it, the blood will flow, and I shall feel the pain. The blood is the same color as yours. God made me, and I am a man.

The case is significant to all of Indian country because the simple fact that it was heard in a court of law changed a long-standing rule that Indians were only three-fifths of a person, and as such not entitled to standing in a court of competent jurisdiction. *When Standing Bear became a man* is how many characterize the case. A history-making precedent for Native people had been established, and for that all Native tribes owe a debt to Standing Bear.

Nevertheless, I have never read a statement more self-aggrandizing and, at the same time, utterly condescending toward Native people. Clearly, according to Judge Dundy, indigenous people in 1879 were at the bottom of the pit of humanity and white people were at the pinnacle. Therefore, the best we poor Natives could do was divest ourselves of all that we were and strive to be part of that "higher civilization."

There are groups throughout the world who maintain a lifestyle that has not given in entirely to a modern technocratic existence. The Mongol reindeer herders, the Sami of Norway who also herd reindeer, the Bushmen of the Kalahari, a few indigenous tribes in the rain forests of Brazil, and even some of the Amish fit into that category. I mention this because there are people who not only survive but also thrive without the so-called advantages of modern technology. Some limit their use of it, and some consciously choose to shun it entirely. That lifestyle, the absence or limited use of technology, would likely not be included in the definition of *civilization*: "the stage of human social development and organization that is considered most advanced." But who is the ultimate and unbiased judge to determine which nation or society fits that definition?

We Americans are quick to declare that we are the "greatest nation" on the planet, possibly the greatest ever. That is a judgment call, and we seem to be the only people making that case. Judge Dundy's perception of American civilization is likewise an ethnocentric opinion. Furthermore, he not only summarily denigrates indigenous people of North America, he also devalues all other developed countries in the world. The Sami, the Bushmen, and the interior tribes of Brazil would likely not fit into Dundy's biased perception of civilization simply because the interpretation of an "advanced" civilization seems largely based on industry, technology, religion, and skin color. Other factors such as human rights, family values, and social equality are not high on the list. Ironically, those factors were of higher priority among Standing Bear's Ponca than they were in Judge Dundy's America, and they are foundational pillars for the Sami, the Bushmen, and the tribes of the Amazon. That is how they survive and thrive, not by technology or modern industry.

In my estimation, Judge Dundy based his opinion on one factor and one factor only: the Ponca were inferior because they were brown-skinned Natives. That was the mindset of white America in the latter part of the nineteenth century, and it was authentically white American thinking.

The question that formed in my mind after I learned of Standing Bear's heroic struggle and the outcome of his trial is one I do not hear or read often: What would Judge Dundy's ruling have been if Standing Bear had not been willing to acculturate to the white American lifestyle? What would have happened if Standing Bear asserted that he would not change?

Part of me wonders if Standing Bear really pulled a fast one on Judge Dundy, purely in the interest of not subjecting his people to further hardship. Perhaps he told his lawyers and Judge Dundy exactly what he knew they wanted to hear, exactly what he knew would appeal to their ethnocentric thinking. If that was the case, then Standing Bear's victory was the epitome of cleverness and he defeated his oppressors without firing a shot, because he appealed to their arrogance. The fact of the matter was that many Native people in many Native communities and reservations may have lived in square houses, worn American clothes, and spoken English, but in their heart of hearts they were Lakota, or Dine, or Anishinabe … or Ponca. As recently as a few years ago, an old Arapaho medicine man on the Wind River Reservation was just such a holdout, if you will, and had been all his life until he died. He spoke very little English, and his lifestyle was guided by his strong sense of identity as an Arapaho.

I can only speculate what Dundy's ruling might have been if Standing Bear had taken a different tack, but my guess is that the judge would not have issued such a generous ruling. My guess is that he would have ordered that Standing Bear and his twenty-eight followers be immediately dispatched back to Indian Territory.

Eleven years later, another white male expressed his sense of white superiority. His name was L. Frank Baum, the author of *The Wizard of Oz*. On December 20, 1890, after the Hunkpapa Lakota medicine man and leader was killed by Indian police, he wrote an editorial in a South Dakota newspaper:

The proud spirit of the original owners of these vast prairies inherited through centuries of fierce and bloody wars for their possession, lingered last in the bosom of Sitting Bull. With his fall the nobility of the Redskin is extinguished, and what few are left are a pack of whining curs who lick the hand that smites them. The Whites, by law of conquest, by justice of civilization, are masters of the American continent, and the best safety of the frontier settlements will be secured by the total annihilation of the few remaining Indians. Why not annihilation? Their glory had fled, their spirit broken, their manhood effaced, better that they die than live the miserable wretches that they are. (December 20, 1890, *Aberdeen Weekend Pioneer*)

Shortly after the Massacre at Wounded Knee on the Pine Ridge Reservation on December 29, 1890, Baum continued his tirade:

The *Pioneer* has before declared that our safety depends upon the total extermination of the Indians. Having wronged them for centuries, we had better in order to protect our civilization, follow it up by one more wrong and wipe these untamed and untamable creatures from the face of the earth. (January 3, 1891, *Aberdeen Weekend Pioneer*)

Judge Dundy's grandiose ethnocentricity was eclipsed by Baum's unabashed racism, but both viewpoints were not that uncommon for the time.

Unfortunately, Judge Dundy's—if not Baum's—mindset prevails to this day and has been given a cruelly punitive twist by a racist president. Consequently, brown-skinned children have been taken away from parents and grandparents as they've crossed the southern US–Mexican border, and then been incarcerated. Reports were that, by the end of 2018, there were between 12,500 and 5,000 children held in jail-like conditions at various locations, and most had not seen their parents or grandparents for weeks. Some of the children were toddlers, or younger. Brown-skinned immigrants cross the southern US border in search of a better life, fleeing from atrocities in their home countries—some, or perhaps many, knowing that the racial attitudes north of the border toward anyone not white might subject them to unforeseen hardships after they cross into the United States. Of course, not all of them are bona fide asylum seekers, but an overwhelming majority of them are, and crossing the border illegally does have its consequences. However, a "nation of laws" has ignored due process that is mandated by law, and young children have borne the brunt of racist actions, very likely emotionally scarring them for life. This sort of action is nothing new, and is authentically the product of a white American mindset. After all, we need only revisit the boarding school era in American history.

Caring and compassionate white people have been alarmed, denouncing the treatment of immigrant children by reminding others that "this is not who we are" or "we are better than this." Those of us who are brown-skinned fervently hope and pray that mainstream America is "better than this," but we must also remind our white compatriots that the treatment of brown-skinned immigrant children in 2019 is exactly *who you are*. Your country has done it before, and as recently as the 1950s. Beginning in the late 1870s with the Carlisle Indian Industrial School, located in Carlisle, Pennsylvania, the boarding school era and its attendant trauma inflicted on generations of Native children of many tribes is a matter of record, but it is sadly ignored by white

America. Native children, many very young, were literally taken out of their mothers' arms.

Those of us who know that history are not surprised that brown-skinned immigrant children are being taken from their parents in 2019. Those who did not learn that history about their own country and about what their own kind did are surprised; some are even shocked. A sad axiom is at work: *Those who do not know history are doomed to repeat it.* However, as white America is repeating a tragic aspect of its history, it is not white American children who are bearing the brunt of that ignorance. Brown-skinned children are. I can only wonder if the history books in the foreseeable future, likely written mostly or only by white historians, will tell the story with all of its cruel reality or if they will veil it, or justify it, or sugarcoat it to protect white sensibilities.

If white Americans are genuinely surprised and shocked by the treatment of brown-skinned immigrants in 2019, it is indicative of two sad realities: one, they do not know the true history of their invasion of North America, and two, they are ignoring that history if they know it, thereby dismissing 2019 as a necessary consequence of Manifest Destiny. When all is said and done, the treatment of brown-skinned immigrants in 2019 is a manifestation of white privilege, indicative of *what white America has been and still is.*

At the same time the sad and tragic events have been occurring on the southern border with Mexico, other immigrants—not brown-skins—were entering or were already in the United States, primarily from Europe and numbering nearly seven hundred thousand—entire families in most cases. Those parents and grandparents did not have their children and grandchildren taken away from them. Furthermore, there were stories of pregnant Russian women traveling to the United States to give birth, likely so their babies could come into the world as American citizens. If the "infestation" of immigrants was such an issue, one can only wonder at the lack of outcry regarding these two instances of "infestation."

As one Native person listening to and watching the news in 2019, I identified with the brown-skinned immigrants and not the American collective, because my kind of brown-skinned people and their kind of brown-skinned people were here on this continent long, long before the people who tore our families apart and are tearing their families apart came to our shores. This reality is the newcomers are in control. They have the social and economic and political power—not to mention the ability to punitively enforce laws and regulations. That is who they are, that is their authenticity.

I suspect that many Native people share my sentiments, and, because of our shared history, that is part of the authenticity of who we are. Furthermore, we Native people must especially be cognizant of the axiom of forgetting history, because—to put it bluntly—we cannot allow the colonizer to repeat the sins committed against our ancestors. We must not allow ourselves to acculturate ourselves to white mainstream society, blissfully ignorant of those sins. If we do, our children and grandchildren may well face the attitudes and actions of white privilege that exacerbated the 2019 immigrant issue at our southern border.

The issue that I wrestle with now is our authenticity as Lakota people today, after observing three generations of Lakota people: mine, my children's, and my grandchildren's—mired in the unrelenting pull of white mainstream culture. Who are we, really?

We are watered-down versions of our ancestors. Some of us physically still resemble our ancestors to varying degrees, and others of us do not. That factor, however, is nowhere near as important as the extent to which we know our culture and history, and the manner in which we live our true Lakota values. If we have been taught who we are as Lakota, and if we believe in who we are, our unavoidable and basically necessary participation in the mainstream culture should be nothing more than another obstacle we have had to adapt to in the course of our journey as an identifiable and viable indigenous nation.

Having said that, here are the issues that are part of our daily lives:

- Holidays. We Lakota people observe the American mainstream holidays, especially Thanksgiving, Christmas, and the Fourth of July—although more and more of us put a different spin on Thanksgiving, and Christmas is largely a secular observance. We have, more or less, incorporated the Fourth of July by having celebrations or pow-wows.

- Foods. Our diet is predominantly white American food, and has been since the late 1860s with the first issuance of government rations, including sugar, coffee, lard, corn, beans, rice, and cattle. A dire consequence of this diet has been the high rate of diabetes among us. Now we are addicted to soda, to convenience, to fast and processed foods, just as much of the general population is.

- Houses. We live in square houses, which is antithetical to the tremendous cultural importance of the circle that is the basis for nearly all Lakota philosophy and spiritual beliefs.

- Elders. We do not revere and respect our elders in the way our ancestors did.

- Values. We are more apt to follow white mainstream customs than our basic Lakota values. A puzzling exam-

ple is the "princess pageant" at nearly every major celebration or pow-wow. Although we decry or ridicule the
historical gaffe of "Indian princesses," we crown many
at each pow-wow and follow the white mainstream custom of objectifying women and girls.

- Materialism. We have become materialistic, transition-
ing from a society that looked after those who were less
fortunate to one with hundreds, if not thousands, of
homeless people.

- Names. We no longer use traditional names as our primary identities. We have Christianized or European
first names and surnames, mandated by the Bureau of
Indian Affairs, thus forcing a patronymic system. And
not all of us have a traditional Lakota name, and those
of us who do are not known by it.

Of course, there are other examples such as the insidiously
strong hold Christianity still has among us. That, along with all
of the previous examples, indicates that we have accepted, or
perhaps cannot avoid the lure of the colonizers and their culture,
nor can we circumvent their continuing influence. And I am
wondering to what extent all of that has affected our authenticity as a culture as well as individual members and participants
in our culture.

That is an issue—if we all agree that it is—that we need to
discuss and give serious thought to. Can we go back to the true
authenticity of the arrow with the stone point and all of its natural components? Crafting an authentic arrow, even in this day
and age, is still possible. But can we Lakota today remake ourselves into what our ancestors were in the era before the invasion
and influence of white people? We cannot, sadly. So perhaps we
are now like the arrow with the iron point: mostly authentic.

There are four major components of a truly authentic Lakota arrow: the shaft, the feathers, sinew, and the stone point. Using that arrow with an iron point as an analogy, only one component is made from something different, meaning three other components are still authentic. I believe that is how we must look at ourselves today. And if we are like that arrow with the iron point, we must strive to maintain as much authenticity as we have left. If we are like that arrow with the iron point, we accept that outside influences have changed us, but not to the point where we are no longer recognizable.

That Lakota arrow with an iron point is still a Lakota arrow. A Lakota person knowledgeable of history and culture and grounded in Lakota philosophies and spiritual beliefs is still a Lakota. That is our new authenticity, but we must ensure that we do not allow it to be further diminished.

Hope

Hope is often the last resort, the last effort we make when all else has failed or fallen short. When the inevitability of an outcome is apparent or when we know the solution or change we want will not happen, we still hope. Hope is the refusal to give in, the refusal to yield.

As our daughters and I watched their mother and my wife waste away from cancer, we still hoped she would recover. I hoped she would rally, in spite of the soul-searing prognosis from two separate oncologists. The disease was well into stage IV when the first diagnosis was given to us. The cold and unyielding reality indicated no chance of recovery, with a life expectancy of four months. Nonetheless, she did not give in to despair, and her hope ignited mine. Even when she slipped into a coma the day before she died, I still hoped, even while I prayed for a merciful end to her pain. Even as I somehow sensed that her spirit was leaving, I still hoped against the inevitable.

We hope for much in life—for a good job, for our team to win, to get the loan to buy a car or a house, for our children to grow up healthy and to turn out well. Not all of those expectations for a certain thing to happen turn out the way we hope. For most of us, our sense of reality tells us there will be disappointment, or loss, but we still hope because it rises from an unwillingness to quit.

Because we hope, we pick ourselves up and keep going, perhaps because a part of us senses that the void of hopelessness is a bottomless pit. But we also sense somehow that hope is our last refuge, that pivotal axis, because hope is either our last stand or a turning point.

We Natives are the smallest ethnically identified minority in the United States. Estimates from various agencies, such as the US Census Bureau and Bureau of Indian Affairs, of the combined tribal population in the United States ranges anywhere from two to three million, less than 1 percent of the general population. Black Americans are 13 percent, Hispanic Americans are 18 percent, and Asian Americans are 6 percent. Our political clout is negligible, therefore we must rely on the honest awareness of other people—mostly white—in order to maintain or gain on any issue regarding our legal, social, educational, and political well-being. But since the United States became a nation, that has been an uphill battle for us. After all, its Constitution refers to us as "merciless Indian Savages." Yet we have little choice but to appeal to the cold heart of the US government on issues that affect us, while hoping that the people represented by it are not as devoid of compassion. We know it is there. The extent of it has always been consistently indeterminable, depending on the issue and the political climate for white Americans. Beginning January 20, 2017, our situation has not been in such jeopardy—in my opinion—since the Reagan administration. It is distressing to us that brown-skinned people appealing to the gentler side of this nation have had their families torn apart and their children incarcerated. Yet, they, and we, continue to hope.

Issues that concern us include (but are not necessarily limited to) health care, education, land loss, further loss of languages and culture, reservation economy, housing, racism, and white privilege. Now and then a singular issue—such as a sports team's mascot—will grab the attention of mainstream America and thrust us into the spotlight, very briefly, and then fade even faster. Another flash-in-the-pan headline grabber happens when the fashion world appropriates Native cultural icons, such as a Plains headdress, for a tasteless, self-aggrandizing display, and then later apologizes for its "inappropriateness." And those kinds of arrogant acts of white privilege will not stop, because a fashion designer or the wealthy owner of a professional sports team will never display sensitivity and compassion toward us as a marginalized minority, because of their arrogance. We are a marginalized minority, and our political, economic, and legal clout is small. All we can do is appeal to the hearts and minds of caring and compassionate white people.

Therein is our hope.

Things were not always this way. There was a time when there was nothing but brown-skinned people on this continent.

White people came with a sense of entitlement because they were white. They began killing brown-skinned people and wolves and changing the environment to serve their needs and comforts. The daunting reality for us brown-skinned people now is that white people will not go away. There are, therefore, two choices we brown-skins face culturally as a consequence of white people's actions and attitudes, as well as our interactions with them, and they are simple yet far-reaching: one, we become like them, or two, we retain our cultures.

Many of our ancestors across many tribes tried living like white people or becoming like them, thereby hoping they would be regarded with kindness and tolerance. I have heard and read stories of the Cherokee people in the early 1800s doing just that. They developed an alphabet in order to write their own language, published their own newspaper, and reportedly organized their towns with streets and alleys. That apparently did not impress President Andrew Jackson, who ordered their removal west to Indian Territory in Oklahoma, an area set aside just for that purpose: discarded Natives. That tragic episode is known as the Trail of Tears, because of the extreme hardships that caused illness and death during long and arduous treks. The Creeks, Seminoles, Choctaws, and Chickasaws were also forcibly removed.

In the long run, it mattered not whether we changed to accommodate them or resisted to maintain our cultures and keep our languages and territory. And perhaps a portent for Native people was an event that is touted as a high-water mark in the history of the white people on this continent.

Europeans claimed Turtle Island/North America by "right of discovery" and essentially divided it among themselves. Not for a second did they consider that the human beings already living here were human beings. The perspective they adopted toward the continent new to them was that they—the Europeans—regarded it as nothing more than a commodity, property to be used as they needed and saw fit. To them, it was something to be feared and something to be used. They feared the vast wilderness and everything that was part of it, which included wolves and Natives. They came and set about claiming the land, altering it to fit their lifestyle, and taking from it to fit their needs and desires, and killing anything that got in the way. That, in a nutshell, is the history of Turtle Island/North America.

Every bit of that tragic history had, and is having, a consequence, and one episode certainly foretold the future for the indigenous peoples who had inhabited this continent for many millennia—the Lewis and Clark voyage of 1804 to 1806, commonly referred to as the Corps of Discovery expedition.

That episode began when the fledgling United States bought a territory claimed by France, essentially the central middle third of the continent. To the French it was Vente de la Louisane, or "Sale of Louisiana." The United States paid fifteen million dollars for 828 thousand square miles of territory thereto largely unknown to Europeans and Euro-Americans. In the history of white America it is known as the Louisiana Purchase, a step in the takeover of an entire continent. If ever there was a racial equivalent to the law of physics that states "to every action there is an opposite and equal reaction," the consequence of this transaction between two white nations was that. In the history of the indigenous people who occupied that part of the continent, it was another step in the process that resulted in the loss of territory, genocide, and the decimation of their lives and cultures. (Prior to 1803, the indigenous tribes east of the Mississippi River had already experienced what those west of the Mississippi were about to face.)

The territory included land that was to form all or parts of several current states: Arkansas, Missouri, Iowa, Oklahoma, Kansas, Nebraska, Minnesota, North and South Dakota, New Mexico, Texas, Montana, Wyoming, Colorado, and two Canadian provinces.

Let us not misunderstand that while the westward expansion of the United States meant the growth and development of the white Euro-American nation, it had the tragically opposite consequence for the at least sixty different indigenous tribes and nations living within the "Louisiana Territory."

President Thomas Jefferson made the purchase in spite of opposition from other politicians and government officials. And once the purchase was made, he saw a need to explore this newly acquired territory. He also wanted to find a practical route across the western half of the continent before other European countries did, both to map it and to establish trade with Indian tribes. To that end he selected his secretary, Meriwether Lewis, to lead an expedition to do just that. Little did he know—or perhaps he did—that he was setting in motion an event that would shape the futures of indigenous peoples to this day.

The "voyage of discovery" is touted in many books and articles, all from the perspective of the explorers. To be sure, there is the usual cursory mention of the tribes that helped in some way, but rarely is there substantial scholarly discourse by non-Native writers and historians about the role of indigenous people in the success of the expedition. Much has been said and written about the contribution of Sacajawea, the young Shoshone woman (a teenager). She was likely captured as a young girl and eventually ended up as a captive and/or wife to French fur trapper Toussaint Charbonneau. She and Charbonneau were among the Mandan, who lived along the Missouri River in present-day south-central North Dakota, when the Lewis and Clark expedition arrived there. When Charbonneau was hired by the expedition, Sacajawea went along with him. She ended up guiding the expedition through territory she knew as a child, and she also brokered a deal with her brother's people for horses, a mode of transportation they sorely needed once they left the river and went overland.

There were at least two Native or part-Native members of the expedition: one was a guide and hunter and the other served as an interpreter. Along with Sacajawea, they were members of the expedition—Sacajawea more or less by default—and their efforts, experience, and knowledge did contribute to its success. But very little is said or written about indigenous tribes who provided food, shelter, and directions. Those who did so directly were the Mandan, the Lemhi Shoshone (Sacajawea's people), the Nez Perce, and the Clatsop. The Mandan allowed the expedition to winter (1804–1805) in their territory, the Lemhi Shoshone and the Nez Perce traded horses and provided food and directions, and the Clatsop allowed them to winter (1805–1806) in their territory along the Oregon coast, as well as provided food.

More than one white writer or historian has touted the Lewis and Clark exploratory journey as the "equivalent in its day of going to the moon and back." There is no denying it was a significant accomplishment, but interestingly one that was not widely applauded until much later. Let us not forget that by the time Europeans learned of the existence of a new continent, the indigenous people of Turtle Island had been settled in and thriving in every part of that continent for thousands of years, a consequence of exodus, migration, and exploration.

Much of the Lewis and Clark expedition's success was due to persistence and adequate planning, but it included a certain amount of good fortune, too—or perhaps it is more accurate to say "just plain dumb luck." What would have happened if Charbonneau and Sacajawea had not been at the Mandan village and Charbonneau had not been hired on? The Corps of Discovery would not have benefited from Sacajawea's knowledge of the territory farther to the west. They might not have successfully traded with her people for horses, if they had even made it that far. What would have happened if they had not had the services of a Native guide through the mountains? What would have happened if they had not been given food when they needed it?

If the Lewis and Clark party had not benefited from the generosity and tolerance of the Native people they had direct contact with, the story very likely would have been one of failure. Or perhaps it would have been an unsolved mystery if they had simply lost their way and disappeared or had starved to death.

History tells us that the Lewis and Clark expedition did plan as much as possible for the task ahead. But at the time Euro-Americans knew very little about the territory President Jefferson had tasked them with exploring. Indeed, there were rumors of woolly mammoths, mountains of salt, and lakes of whiskey in the vast lands to the west. And they knew next to nothing of the indigenous nations west of the Mississippi. Furthermore, their racial attitudes toward Native people—Indians—were based on what they knew of Native peoples east of the Mississippi. By 1800, many tribes had been decimated by disease or had moved away from white enclaves, and whites by and large regarded Natives as a subjugated or conquered people. Furthermore, Lewis and Clark had virtually no knowledge of the tribes to the west and no idea whether they would be friendly or hostile. The fact that they started and proceeded on their journey in spite of that had as much to do with naivete and a sense of racial superiority as it did with commitment to their mission.

Along the route of the Corps of Discovery, from Camp Dubois in Missouri to the Oregon Coast, much of it on the Missouri River, they traveled through the territories of at least forty to sixty different tribes. From beginning to end they had direct contact with at least nine groups or tribes—Otoe, Dakota, Lakota, Mandan, Salish (Flathead), Shoshone, Nez Perce, Clatsop, and Pikani (Blackfeet). Some of those direct contacts were friendly, most were tolerant, some were indifferent, and at least two were hostile. Contact occurred because it could not be avoided or because the expedition needed something, whether it was unimpeded passage, food, simple directions, or—as in the case of the Mandan—a place to shelter for the winter.

As it turned out, the food did run out, the expedition lost their way, they needed horses to travel overland, and there was nowhere to obtain those necessities but from the Natives of the area—people they were generally suspicious of or considered inferior. Unless, of course, these thirty white people (excluding Sacajawea, her half-Shoshone infant son, and Clark's slave, York) were somehow exempt from or above the prevailing white attitudes of the time toward Natives—or Indians.

Desperation, especially when driven by cold and hunger, is a powerful motivator, overcoming barriers of fear, suspicion, and mistrust in the course of human interaction. And yet even such a powerful motivator often needs the impetus of another human feeling—hope.

Thirty-three people—thirty of them white—facing starvation, bone-chilling cold, and one mountain range after another in what they likely perceived to be a friendless land, had to have known a feeling of desperation, especially when the means to find food, warmth, and the right trail seemed impossible to obtain. And when they could not mitigate the obstacles themselves and provide for themselves, there was no choice but to look to hope and reach out to those who could help—and that certainly was not other white people.

Anyone in desperate need reaches out to hope and in hope of finding an answer and fulfilling a need. Hope, in my opinion, more than any other human state, feeling, or condition, diminishes fear, suspicion, and mistrust. Desperation does awaken hope.

If the members of the Lewis and Clark expedition, the very human members, had not reached out with hope in spite of their fears, their suspicions, and their mistrust of anyone not white, their journey would very likely have ended ignominiously.

I like to think that the members of the expedition reached out in hope in spite of their racial prejudices, as opposed to reaching out with a sense of entitlement *because* of their racial prejudices. But the fact of the matter is they had very little choice but to trust to hope on more than one occasion, and that hope was not misplaced. The people they feared and even looked down upon came to their aid.

As a student of history I must look at this event, the Lewis and Clark expedition, as one part in the broader context of the history of the indigenous peoples of Turtle Island and their interaction with Europeans and Euro-Americans. Overall, it was probably more positive than most.

Someone said there is no such thing as "human nature" because each group of people has its own whims, habits, tendencies, proclivities, and attitudes toward and about everything and everyone. It follows then, that within that context of Turtle Island/

North American history, white people acted from the "nature" of who and what they were, and are, just as Native people did, and do. Unfortunately, much, if not most, of the interaction between the indigenous people of this continent of Turtle Island and the immigrants from Europe was ugly and confrontational. And although the Lewis and Clark expedition was, with the exception of two incidents, not confrontational, it was in that broader context still an invasion, and it set the stage for the ugly and confrontational occurrences that were to come later. I use it here to show that for any individual and any group of people, hope is often the last ally, and no one is exempt from relying on hope—even those who think themselves invincible or righteous or entitled. Hope, perhaps, is the one thing that can enable, or force, people to step outside of their own "natures," as it were. Therein is a lesson for all of us. No one is exempt from relying on hope.

That interaction between the indigenous people of Turtle Island and the European immigrants is still happening. In the broadest context possible, the roles have been reversed, so to speak. The immigrants came here needy and landless, and now they own the land and we are needy and landless. As Vine Deloria, Jr. wrote: "In the beginning we had the land and they had the Book. Now we have the Book and they have the land." No truer or sadder words were ever spoken or written.

What we face, the indigenous or Native tribes and nations that still exist, are ethnocentric, paternalistic governments in the United States and Canada whose actions and policies toward us are largely supported by white mainstream societies or enabled by their apathy and/or ignorance. This is not to say, however, that there are not Euro-Americans, white people, who sympathize and support us. Thankfully there are, and some have literally stood with us. Therein lies hope.

In my personal and professional life and in my travels throughout this country, I have met those kinds of people. Some have helped me personally and professionally—as one human being to another, and not as a white person helping an Indian. They have taught me an important and valuable lesson: that while I may have the right to criticize and indict an entire group (or race) of people for the horrific realities of human history on this continent during the past five hundred years, there are the few within that group who abhor what happened and grieve over it. And they are in many walks of life, as teachers, clerics, writers, social activists, auto mechanics, lawyers, and even editors and publishers (to list but a few), and they are rich and poor, influential and ordinary. But no matter who they are and what their station in life is, they have something in common—a yearning for the truth where history is concerned, and a sense of fairness and compassion. Therein lies hope.

There is a lesson for all of us in the Lewis and Clark experience, and that comes from what did not, but could very well have happened. Those explorers traveled through the territories of, at the very least, forty tribes. And at any point any of those tribes could have rightfully regarded the group as invaders and taken military action. It almost happened near the Bad River in what is now South Dakota when an incident escalated to the point that my ancestors, the Sicangu Lakota, and the Lewis and Clark party were facing each other with weapons drawn. Of course, the reasons for that incident are told differently from each side. The explorers accused a few young Lakota men of attempting to take a boat or goods as toll for passage along the Missouri River, while there are stories among the Sicangu that say the whites attempted to take a hostage to ensure safe passage. In any case, a leader among the Lakota gave the order to stand down. While the explorers boasted they could have emerged victorious, if the bullets and the arrows had flown, both sides would have suffered casualties, and the Lewis and Clark expedition might well have ended at Bad River. (Suffice to say that Clark characterized my ancestors as "the vilest miscreants of the savage race" because of that incident.) Or, if a series of confrontations had occurred along the route, Lewis and Clark would have lost both men and supplies. All in all, more than one tribal group could have taken hostile action against the explorers, but not one did. That is but one small part of Turtle Island/North America's history as Natives and immigrants, and yet it does reveal possibilities for positive consequences if we choose to follow the less traveled road of tolerance rather than the too often crowded path of conflict.

Therefore, I place my hope in two groups of people, and one is the non-Native segment of our mainstream population (in the United States and Canada) who truly care about the welfare of others, and a large portion of that hope is placed in white people who understand what white privilege is about and who, I hope, make an effort to circumvent it.

I hope that enough white people learn the real history of this continent, even though it is an ugly history, and take steps to ensure that the true history of white and Native interaction be taught to all Americans. To create a realistic awareness of the past is to guarantee that all the ugly things do not happen again, ever. I hope that white people learn and understand that genocide and slavery are the great sins of their ancestors. And it is their contemporary sin if they cannot or do not accept that reality.

Rarely has anyone (or any group) who asked for mercy from those oppressing them given mercy or quarter. In spite of this, we as Native people must hope that there is compassion and goodness in white society for the marginalized and oppressed. We must place our hope in the people, not the government or its elected leaders—because elected "leaders" are politicians, and they are the ones who created the problems and who then tell us they are working to find solutions in order to help us, even though the problem could have been avoided in the first place. I, for one, will place that hope and extend it to the cosmos, because where there is one good person and one kind heart, surely there are others.

My greatest hope is in the next generation of Native people of all the tribes and nations, the next generation of descendants of the original inhabitants of Turtle Island, but most especially in the Lakota. I hope that the coming generations of Lakota learn all of their history and incorporate their culture into their daily lives. I hope they learn their language, first to revive it and then strengthen it by ensuring that it is taught in Lakota homes and within Lakota families, communities, and schools.

And, finally, I will close with a story to remind those of us who are Lakota that throughout our history we have faced tough situations, sometimes indescribably so, and we are still here. I know many of us who are Sicangu know this story.

The seven groups or bands of the Lakota each have a name that speaks to a characteristic or an event. The name *Sicangu* (see-chan-guh, the last syllable is often called a guttural sound) means "burnt thigh." There is a story of how that name was earned, and here is the version I heard as a child.

Long ago, sometime after our people came to the plains, some stayed east of the Great Muddy (Missouri) River, and some crossed and went west. This was the time before horses, and even so, because the numberless herds of *pte* (pteh) or *tatanka* (thah-tan-kah), the bison or buffalo, on which the people came to depend for food, shelter, and clothing, were nomadic, the people became nomadic as well. Not only did they follow certain herds, they also moved their villages to adjust to weather patterns or the change of seasons.

A small village was moving one autumn day, going from west to east. Everyone walked, of course; some of their personal and family possessions were on their backs and some were pulled by the large dogs using drag poles, onto which bundles and containers were loaded. Every village was a group or groups of extended families, so there was a mixture of age groups ranging from the very young to elders.

In the autumn it was not unusual for great storm clouds, thunderheads, to gather in the west, especially late in the day. Sometimes they evolved into storms with wind and rain, and sometimes they did little more than growl with thunder. On this occasion, as the village of people walked across the prairie, there was thunder and lightning in the clouds west of them, and a bit of wind. And, as luck would have it, lightning struck the dry autumn grass and started a small fire. The people were not overly concerned until the breezes turned to pushy winds, fanning the flames and driving them east.

The people hurried to find safety, which meant getting to some body of water. In that part of the prairie lands water meant at least a creek, but even a wet bog would have provided some level of safety. On this day, though, none could be found, so the only recourse was to move away from the growing fire as quickly as possible. Alarmingly, however, the winds increased and the flames grew higher and faster.

Living on the plains, the people knew that lightning-sparked fires were part of their reality, so the phenomenon was nothing new. Nevertheless, this group was chased by flames that were growing larger and more intense with each gust of wind. Furthermore, they could only move as fast as the slowest among them. Soon it was all too apparent that they could not outrun the oncoming prairie fire.

All the dogs were relieved of their burdens and set free, and it is said that many of the elders advised the younger ones to leave them and run to safety. Many of the parents poured the water carried in buffalo bladder flasks on their children. Such measures of desperation are taken when something disastrous is inevitable. People prayed and sang songs to encourage others, but all seemed lost.

It is said that an old woman spoke up then, advising that the only chance for some of them to survive was to run back through the flames. Most thought it was a ridiculous suggestion, but some saw some logic in the old woman's words. There were those who decided to run away from the rapidly advancing fire, but a few stayed to take their chances with the old woman. Divesting themselves of clothing and other items that would instantly catch fire, they followed the old woman's advice and ran into the flames.

We cannot know how wide the fire was from front to back, but we do know that some people did make it through, although there were casualties. The first to succumb to the heat and flames were the very old and the very young. Those who made it through from one side to the other, through the unimaginably intense heat, suffered the pain of horrible burns and, of course, were scarred. Many of the worst scars were on legs and thighs.

Thereafter, the people called themselves The Burnt Thigh People.

If there was ever a situation where all that was left was hope, this was it. It was the hope of survival, the hope of not dying horribly that had to have compelled our ancestors through the fire. To me, that speaks to the power of hope.

My beloved wife did die in spite of her hope, in spite of mine. But must that mean that I should forever disdain hope? I think not, and one reason is that she dared to hope in the face of overwhelming odds, and thereby taught me that we must never abandon hope. The people who faced the flames on that prairie so long ago did not abandon hope, and it was hope that gave them the strength to run into the fire.

And our history is such that some of us are the fire, and a few of us are the survivors, and survivors know the power of hope.

The Pipeline Protests
Their Insignificance to Mainstream America

Not since Wounded Knee in 1973 has an issue involving Native people captured the nation and the world's attention the way the protest against the Dakota Access Pipeline (DAPL) did in 2016 and 2017. If it had not been for social media, however, the pipeline would have flown under the radar. There were several facets to that phenomenon, but arguably the three most obvious were Native unity, racism against Natives, and white privilege. There were also many subsets and darker stories that were part of the larger narrative, some true and some not. But all of it put Native people, albeit briefly, on the world stage.

The event is over, the camp was taken down, and people have gone back to their homes and lives, but I am certain many of us are still pondering and debating what it was exactly that happened on that meadow and on those hills near the Cannonball River.

I am not wise enough to analyze events and draw comprehensive social or legal conclusions, or predict what it might mean in the future for the people and the issues that were part of the total experience. But as one who was an observer for part of the time, I can only express my reaction to the DAPL protest and how it affected me.

Two factors resonated deeply with me: the number of people who came to Standing Rock to be part of it and the number of different Native tribes that were represented. Estimates of the number of people in the camps varied somewhat, but some were as high as ten thousand. It is a good bet that someone has a fairly accurate estimate, and I would guess it would be those people in the light planes that circled the camp, flying low and slow. (On at least two of those planes I did not see an aircraft identification number on the fuselage.) My gut-prompted guess is between four and five thousand. Of course, it was a fluid population in that people were arriving and leaving constantly. Numbers increased on the weekends as many tribal members in the region drove in to join the encampment. Suffice to say everyone who was part of the experience, for one or a few days or for many, felt the sense of unity and a connection with others there—though they might have known or been acquainted with only a few.

One of the most stirring sights for me was the display of tribal flags—hundreds of them. And the thought and the comment that was the topic of many conversations was, more or less: "Not since Little Bighorn in 1876 have so many of us come together to fight for a cause."

I can state unequivocally that I have never seen so many Native people from so many different tribes together in one place. Perhaps in a sense it was similar to what the Lakota, Northern Cheyenne, and Arapaho people felt at the Greasy Grass encampment in 1876. In their case, it was not the number of different tribal nations but rather the sheer number of people in one place—estimates range from eight to ten thousand. And, of course, somewhere between ten to fifteen thousand horses. At Standing Rock, vehicles replaced the horses, of which there were likely several hundred. And there is one definite and defining similarity between the DAPL protest camp and our ancestors at

Greasy Grass—a sense of unity. Many or perhaps all of us tribal members who were there, whether for a few hours, a few days, or for the duration, felt that sense of unity.

Each time I wandered through the camps—the main one on the north side of the river and the Sicangu camp on the south side—I was struck by the fact that of the hundreds of people I saw, I actually knew or was acquainted with only a few. Overall, although I only camped a few nights, I met fewer than twenty people I knew. Whether we all knew each other or not, one fact was indisputable: all of us had a reason to be there. Perhaps it was just plain curiosity, or to further a cause, to make a stand, to make money, to provide food and water and other necessities or support in the form of labor...

There was an overarching reason the Lakota and their allies came together at the Greasy Grass in 1876, and that was the invasion of white people into Native territories and Native lives. At that point, white people were already firmly established in Lakota territory. The scary and portentous Oregon Trail phenomenon had come and gone as an event, but the implications for our Lakota ancestors (and other tribes) were already manifesting. The army's 1874 expedition into the Black Hills had confirmed the rumor of gold and accelerated the invasion of whites, resulting in an "agreement" in 1875 that removed the western third of the "Great Sioux Reservation." That portion, of course, included the Black Hills. Further, the Sand Creek Massacre of 1864 was still fresh in the minds of the Arapaho, strong allies of the Lakota. These were only two of the tough issues that strengthened the Lakota, Northern Cheyenne, and Northern Arapaho alliance and were among the reasons they responded in 1875 to Sitting Bull's call to gather. That response resulted in the initial gathering at the Chalk Buttes in what is now eastern Montana, and, of course, led to the encampment along the Greasy Grass (Little Bighorn) River several weeks later.

The overarching reason for the protest camp in 2016 and 2017 was to stop the Dakota Access Pipeline because of its possible harm to the environment, especially since there were plans for it to cross *under* the Missouri River. Needless to say, any possibility—the probability, according to many Native people—of leakage was too much of a risk to the land and water. And for me, there was (and is) a tough historical perspective: the threat brought by the white people in the mid-1800s has obviously not gone away or been mitigated to any extent, having been manifested once again by the Dakota Access Pipeline.

From the 1840s to the 1860s, use of the Oregon Trail had a direct adverse impact on the physical environment along its route from Missouri to California and Oregon, in addition to the threat brought by the white people themselves with their attitude of Manifest Destiny. In the thinking of white people, they were *meant* to take over and control an entire continent and bring their lifestyle and "civilization" with them. In the process of accomplishing that, they destroyed in whole or in part hundreds of Native cultures and tribal nations. The DAPL is simply a continuation of the subjugation and rape of the natural environment and its resources to enhance and benefit mainstream white culture, no matter the probability of harm to the land and water or to marginalized people. In this instance, however, the financial benefit from the pipeline is exclusively for oil interests, and not society at large. Furthermore, just as the white migration along the Oregon Trail resulted in trampling the lives and futures of Native people, the DAPL disregards the concerns of Native people, and desecrates ancient burial sites as well. In other words, for us nothing has really changed in all the years since the Oregon Trail. It was, for us, business as usual, and it brings to mind a metaphor applied to the "races" of humans.

Several years ago I heard a young Hidatsa medicine man compare each of the races of humankind to one of the four elements: water, air, earth, and fire. In his opinion, white people are a metaphor for the destructive characteristics of fire. Frankly, I agree because of the destructive consequences of hundreds of years of white colonialism all over the planet. The most obvious consequence is white Europeans' pattern of altering the physical environment to suit their lifestyle, or as some indigenous people characterize it, the "square houses and roads syndrome."

A few years back I asked a group of mostly Native students in a class to guess the location of a scene in a photograph of small shops on either side of a cobblestone street. All of them responded with—more or less—"someplace in Europe." As a matter of fact, it was a small town in New England. As unscientific and subjective as that simple exercise might have been, the point of the discussion in that class was the difference between the characteristics of European colonialism and the ability of indigenous peoples in North America to adapt and fit into the natural environment. Perhaps the darker, or darkest, side of European colonialism throughout history is the *attitude of arrogance and entitlement* that manifests in the alteration, abuse, destruction, and depletion of the physical environment and its resources. Attitude obviously drives actions, and actions have consequences. That reality was manifested in a very personal way for me when I was a boy.

Some of the happiest and most informative years of my childhood happened on a grassy plateau above and east and south of a bend in the Little White River on (what was then) the northern part of the Rosebud Reservation. My grandparents referred to the river as the *Maka Izita* or *Makizita*, which is "Smoking Earth" in Lakota. The most fortunate reality for me was to have been raised by my maternal grandparents—not to mention a few years spent with my paternal grandparents as well. Both sets of grandparents provided amazing insight into the history and culture of our Lakota ancestors.

One late spring on that plateau on the quarter section of land where my maternal grandparents and I lived, I witnessed and learned of two diametrically opposed cultural viewpoints regarding the natural environment. I accompanied my grandfather as we walked the northern part of the east–west fence line around the acreage. This was because a neighboring white rancher was leasing and using the adjacent tribally owned land to the north to pasture his cattle for the summer. My grandfather did not want cattle to push through loose wire and come into our pasture. Just above the gully with the well that was our water source, we found downed wire and a meadowlark's nest in a low thicket of chokecherry shrubs. The shrubs were nothing more than a small, new thicket, only a few years old. In one of the stalks was a new nest. Meadowlarks usually built their nests on the ground in thick grass, so this nest was unusual. Not only that, but the shrubs had grown in the fence line.

We walked back to our house, about a quarter of a mile, and brought back a post and tools to dig a posthole. Back on site, my grandfather dug the hole no more than eighteen inches beyond the fence line, rerouting the wire around the chokecherry shrubs with the meadowlark nest, with its three small speckled eggs. The post also helped to tighten the three strands of barbed wire. Finishing that, we proceeded to inspect the entire remaining half mile of fence and tightened the wire in a few more spots, thus ensuring that our neighbor's cattle would not stray into our pasture.

A few days later the rancher also checked the fence line, a prelude to driving the cattle into the leased pasture adjacent to ours. He was driving the fence line in a small tractor with a blade on the back. From our house I noticed that he stopped at that same spot where we had repaired the fence a few days earlier. Although I did not have a full view of his activity, I heard his tractor as he worked. The next day I decided to walk to the repair site, and I was shocked and saddened by what I discovered. The small chokecherry shrubs were gone, apparently scraped away according to the telltale marks I saw on the ground. Furthermore, the shrubs and the nest had been flattened, probably by the large rear wheels of a tractor. For years after the incident I was bothered by what had apparently happened: the rancher had destroyed the shrubs and the nest to repair the fence. I can understand wanting to repair the fence, but I could not understand why the nest and its eggs had to be destroyed.

I am not in any way implying that that rancher was a bad person simply because he repaired a fence. What I can assume is that he acted according to the values that he learned from his family and his culture. To him it was probably not an issue of right or wrong, but he still had no compassion for the meadowlark nest and its eggs. Those factors likely did not occupy more than a split second of his awareness. The prevailing inclination and thought for him was that keeping his cattle inside the fences of his rented pasture was most important, and therefore he was entitled and obligated to keep the barbed wire tight and the fence line straight. The consequence of that entitlement—the destruction of chokecherry shrubs and a meadowlark's nest—was no concern of his. Which was not unlike the Dakota Access Pipeline using whatever entitlements were available or could be bought in order to move tar sand oil to benefit a corporation.

Years after that fence line incident, it became for me the enduring example of opposing attitudes regarding the natural environment: indigenous adaptability on one hand and arrogant entitlement on the other. Both have consequences—virtually no harm from one and irreparable harm from the other. Those, for me, were the forces that collided at the Dakota Access Pipeline, and affirmed the Hidatsa medicine man's assertion that white Europeans manifest the worst consequences of fire.

That young medicine man also asserted that indigenous people the world over—and certainly on this continent of Turtle Island/North America—were most connected to the Earth. Generally speaking, for most indigenous peoples, our system of spiritual beliefs, rituals, and traditions is entirely based on our relationship to and with the natural world. To put it another way, indigenous traditional spiritual lifestyles are based on the realities of that relationship to and with the natural world, not on a belief in a monotheistic deity and obedience and subservience to it. Indigenous beliefs and the practices are a lifestyle, not a religion. There is not an indigenous "religion"—certainly not for the Lakota.

Perhaps the most profound affirmation of that reality is in a statement spoken in a Lakota prayer. One respectful acknowledgment is to Grandmother Earth. The statement is simple: "To you we shall return." Our relationship to and with Grandmother Earth, at least for those Lakota who follow traditional beliefs, is a real and operative part of our lives. That relationship involves defending Grandmother Earth, though not because she is a commodity and our property is threatened, but rather because to us she is a living and breathing entity, the source of our life as humans. It is from her we came, and to her we shall return when our lives are over.

There is also an affirmation in one of the Lakota traditional ceremonies still practiced—the *Inipi*. It is a rebirth, cleansing, and renewal ritual conducted inside a low, dome-shaped lodge. The ceremony is also more commonly known as a "sweat" because it is essentially a wet sauna. The requisite components are both tangible and intangible. Humility and respect are two, and the connection to Grandmother Earth and the overall reality of the physical world are in the necessary use of earth, air, fire, and water.

The earth is represented in the sweat ceremony by the heated stones that are placed in the center pit of the lodge. Air, of course, is omnipresent, and fire heats the stones before they are carried in to the pit. Finally, water is poured over the red-hot stones to generate the steam and the intense heat.

Traditional Lakota beliefs do incorporate the realities of our place as humans within the broad and all-encompassing spectrum of the physical world around us. Those beliefs are still known and incorporated into our thinking and lifestyles today. Given that reality, it is then understandable that we would oppose the Dakota Access Pipeline because it is a threat to the Earth, that physical environment that is a relative to us, and not a commodity to be used, abused, polluted, and depleted. Furthermore, other tribes and indigenous groups share some of the same basic beliefs and have the same relationship to the Earth, hence the presence and participation of many different tribal nations at the protest camps.

People at the camps who were opposed to the pipeline generally had two reasons: one was the fact that the pipeline was rerouted farther away from Bismarck, North Dakota, after city leaders likely expressed fears of leakage and contamination; the other was that it was close to tribal lands and communities. And even though tribal people and leaders expressed the same concerns, those concerns were not given the same credibility. In short, the city leaders of Bismarck had more political clout (or had perfected the art of cronyism) than the Lakota tribes. Another factor that instigated the protest and one that incensed Native peoples (and still does) was the ludicrous plan to put the pipeline under the Missouri River. It seemed to most Lakota that white people ignored the possible consequence for all people and communities downriver from the pipeline if it leaked into the water. We were, and continue to be, opposed to routing the pipeline under the river, not because any leakage would affect only Native people, but because the consequences would be dire for everyone, foremost for the water.

For most of the non-Native public who saw any of the sketchy and often misleading news about the pipeline protest, the situation might have appeared or was reported as simply a case of *us*, the Native people, against *them*, white law enforcement. And certainly for many white folks in South and North Dakota, it was nothing more. To them, the issue was irrelevant. The whole situation was nothing more than Native people misbehaving. It did not matter to most non-Native people that we were—and continue to be—scared for the environment, and that our rights (especially) under the Fort Laramie Treaty of 1851 were ignored. Furthermore, the reaction of the state of North Dakota was tragically similar to the federal government's reaction to the Ghost Dance Movement in 1890. That reaction was also a misinterpretation of the facts.

In the late 1890s, the situation for the Lakota was dire, and this is a vast understatement. Our ancestors lived under the total control of the federal government, with that control exercised on the local level by the Bureau of Indian Affairs (BIA). By then, the seven Lakota bands were more or less located on or in the area of the current reservations, and all were totally dependent on the annuities provided to them—basically beef, rice, beans, sugar, and coffee. Lakota families were relegated to stand in line once a month to receive them, and limited supplies and unavailability were frequent. There was very little or no hope for change and improvement to these tough and humiliating circumstances. Furthermore, this was true for many Native tribes across the West.

It was then that word came from the Southwest, offering a spark of hope. A Paiute holy man, Wovoka, had experienced a vision wherein he saw a return to the lifestyles enjoyed by Native people before the coming of white people. In order to manifest that vision, the people—Wovoka said—had but to pray to their ancestors and dance. Thus the "Ghost Dance" label came about.

The Lakota sent representatives to the Southwest to hear Wovoka's message and to learn the dances. They returned to their homelands and spread the message, and our ancestors responded in droves. Any opportunity for change, to mitigate the debilitating life under white control, was welcome, especially if it meant a basically peaceful process. Consequently, the Ghost Dance spread like wildfire across the Lakota reservations. Hundreds and even thousands of men, women, and children participated.

The BIA was alarmed by the number of participants and the frequency of the gatherings. They were extremely fearful that armed confrontations would occur, and one Indian Agent in particular—the white administrator of the Pine Ridge agency—wrote letters filled with panic and impending doom, and asked for military protection. Consequently, the War Department responded and sent troops, and ironically the main body was the 7th Cavalry Regiment, the unit that had suffered a decisive defeat at the hands of the Lakota and Northern Cheyenne on the Little Bighorn River, fourteen years earlier. Erroneous assessment of the situation was a direct consequence of the BIA being convinced that the worst possible scenario would occur—armed conflict. Therefore, the government responded with overwhelming force.

The government's flawed assessment and show of force brought about two tragic consequences, occurring two weeks apart. First was the murder of the Hunkpapa Lakota leader and medicine man, Sitting Bull, on December 15, 1890, at his home on the Standing Rock Reservation. Lakota police working for the BIA were sent to arrest him, backed up by army troops. Predictably, circumstances went awry during the arrest attempt and the beloved holy man was killed by his own kind—the Lakota police officers. Second was the infamous Wounded Knee Massacre on December 29, 1890, on the Pine Ridge Reservation. A Mniconju Lakota leader known as Big Foot was fleeing south from the Cheyenne River Reservation to Pine Ridge. Most of his people were women, children, and elderly. The 7th Cavalry, under the command of Colonel James W. Forsyth, intercepted them and escorted them to Wounded Knee Creek, fifteen miles west of the Pine Ridge Agency on December 28. The next morning, during a search for weapons, a shot was fired, and the soldiers opened fire with small arms and with four Hotchkiss artillery guns. The Hotchkiss guns fired 20 millimeter rounds at a rapid rate. When the firing finally stopped, about three hundred Lakota, mostly women and children, had been killed.

Both tragic events can be attributed to the government's misunderstanding of the circumstances surrounding the Ghost Dance, or their conscious decision to ignore the facts, and a willingness to use overwhelming force against the Lakota. Insofar as we know, there was not a single attempt to negotiate with Lakota leaders in hopes of bringing about a peaceful solution. Neither did they give credence to assurances from Lakota leaders that the Ghost Dance was not a threat to the safety of the white people on or near the reservations.

The protests against the DAPL at Standing Rock were peaceful. As far as I know, any of the clashes that occurred were not instigated by overt acts of aggression by the protestors. Nevertheless, the state of North Dakota's immediate response was an armed police presence that soon escalated into what was essentially a military response, given the types of weapons and other equipment and "assets" brought to bear, including body armor, water cannons, and attack dogs.

For me, there were too many similarities between Wounded Knee of 1890 and the DAPL protests of 2016 and 2017. Fortunately, the heavily armed police did not open fire the way the 7th Cavalry did in 1890, although it is entirely possible a few of them might have been so inclined. The horrific and inhumane actions of the 7th Cavalry at Wounded Knee were taken out of a need for revenge (for Little Bighorn) and from a position of absolute impunity. The actions of the law enforcement officers and contracted security at the DAPL protests were sanctioned by all government agencies involved, no matter how egregious they were. At Wounded Knee 1890, the white government and white society did not punish white soldiers for killing unarmed Lakota, mostly women and children. As a matter of fact, eighteen Medals of Honor were awarded. At DAPL 2016–2017, law enforcement officers acted with absolute impunity. The white state and federal governments did not punish or even reprimand law enforcement personnel for excessive use of force against Native protestors. Wounded Knee 1890 was open season on the Lakota, and DAPL 2016–2017 was open season on Natives.

That, then, begs the question regarding race relations in this country: How far have we progressed? Or is it also fair to ask: How far backward have we gone? A terrifying and sickening reality is the common thread linking Wounded Knee 1890 and DAPL 2016–2017: white people in a white society with a government controlled by white people can do as they please to people with brown skin. After all, what reaction will come that is more than a strongly worded condemnation? What, then, is the difference between a white police officer shooting and killing a twelve-year-old Black child and white law enforcement officers at the DAPL protests using water cannons, pepper spray, and attack dogs against brown-skinned people? Legally speaking, none. In each instance the action was taken with the absolute guarantee of impunity, because legality is a matter of power, not a matter of justice.

The actions of the state of North Dakota, aided and abetted by the federal government and other states, were not that of a governmental entity on a mission to solve a problem fairly and justly by giving due consideration to all the facts relevant to the circumstance. They were the actions of a bully intent on ignoring the voices and rights of brown-skinned citizens of the United States, and crushing them physically, psychologically, socially, and politically by using white interpretation, application, and fabrication of law.

Legality is a matter of power, not a matter of justice.

The flip side of the sense of empowerment and unity felt by the Native people at the DAPL gathering was the unmitigated display of racism and white privilege. Those persistent realities have been part of Native life since first contact with Europeans and Euro-Americans. That is nothing new, but the blatant display at the DAPL protest was a frightening reminder that little, if anything, has changed in Native–white relations. The actions of white law enforcement at DAPL were to both crush the protest and intimidate us, pointedly serving to remind us that the federal, state, and local governments do not include us in the phrase "government of the people, by the people, for the people"—only as objects of subjugation in "government of the people."

For us to decry the injustice, unfairness, racism, and white privilege is nothing new to white society at large, and perhaps those cries are heard by most non-Native people as little more than the "sky is falling." But we who suffer the sting of injustice, unfairness, racism, and white privilege must continue to point them out, from the depths of our pain and despair, if necessary, because when did the purveyor of injustice ever admit to its own sins and correct its own attitudes, actions, and policies in any meaningful way without understanding the pain of those oppressed?

For me, those who came to Standing Rock to stand up to injustice, unfairness, racism, and white privilege represented the spiritual strength of all people the world over who have felt the sting of oppressive colonialism. Those who reacted to our resilience with their worst represented the basest instinct of colonialism. No one who came there to stand up for the environment wants the pipeline to leak and poison the land and the water in order to say, "I told you so." What we do want is for others to learn that coexisting with the environment and adapting to it is the way to ensure that our children and grandchildren of any race and color will have an unpolluted environment. We would like the world to understand that there are ways to relate to the natural environment other than to "have dominion" over it to the point of irreparable harm. We want others to learn that the natural environment—Grandmother Earth—is a living entity and not just a commodity to be used and abused for the economic benefit of a few. When a rich white man states that "water is not a human right," then what follows is people dying of thirst because they cannot afford to pay for it.

Several years ago, students in a writing class at Sinte Gleska University brought up the topic of the Keystone XL (KXL) pipeline, and asked me if I thought it would be built. My answer was that it was only a matter of time before enough people who saw the Earth's resources only as a way to make money would be elected to the US Congress, and the wrong person would be elected president. Those people would change the laws and remove the regulations that protect the environment.

The KXL and DAPL are only two pipe of many pipelines. An alarming fact is that there is virtually no pipeline that does not spring a leak and contaminate land and water to some extent.

But the prevailing attitude in this country seems to be the acceptance of some leakage as part and parcel of pipelines, so long as it does not occur on our land or in our backyard. It is not our problem until our land and our backyard are contaminated. My question is: How many backyards must be contaminated before we realize that it is all the same problem? How long before we realize that, as humans, we are of the Earth because we need the resources it provides in order to live and function each and every day. Without air we will suffocate. Without water we will literally shrivel up and die. Without food we will die. Those are necessities provided by the Earth; they do not magically appear in plastic wrappings or bottles for us to buy. Most of the world's human population defines providing for their families as having the money to purchase necessities.

No matter what our religion, our race and ethnicity, the size of our bank accounts, or where we live, we all need air, water, and food in order to live and breathe and function each and every day. A human can survive at least four or five days without water before he or she begins to die. We can survive at least thirty days without food before we begin to die. Without air we will suffocate in minutes. A rich white man will die eventually without those necessities just as surely as a poor Native.

As humans, no matter our race, color, creed, sexual orientation, religion, or economic status, we have much in common that we sadly choose to ignore. We focus instead on skin color. Or to put it bluntly, white-skinned people look down on people with darker skin color. From my perspective, white people have convinced themselves that they are racially, intellectually, and morally superior, when in reality their attitude of disdain and condescension and superiority is a consequence of imperialism and colonialism. And those attitudes and characteristics honed by centuries of conflict and conquest have been ingrained into the psyche of the perpetrator, just as the sense of connection to

Grandmother Earth has been ingrained into those of us who are the original inhabitants of Turtle Island. These two diametrically opposed learned behaviors and racial value systems were on full display at the pipeline protests.

The events there were, for us—the indigenous people who faced the water cannons, pepper spray, and attack dogs—about the air, land, and water, and for them—the white-skinned people who blasted the water cannons and pepper spray and came with their attack dogs—it was about perpetuating colonialism. Therefore, one is led to conclude that not much has changed in this world of ours. One is further led to conclude that the issues and problems we face together—no matter our race, creed, color, sexual orientation, or religion—are not faced with a sense of commonality but rather from the positions of power and powerlessness. In that case, there can be no solution that is fair to us all, but only to the advantage of those in power. For me, that is the sad lesson from Standing Rock.

However, there is an enduring lesson. The reason so many of the people of Turtle Island came to Standing Rock is because we are still the people of Turtle Island. And if we had forgotten, we reminded ourselves that we can be strong together. That is what I choose to take away from Standing Rock.

The Ones Who Came to Dance

Oliver Red Lance opened his sketchbook and revealed two portraits to Johnson Black Horn. He put them side-by-side on the kitchen table. For a moment the medicine man ignored the artist and gazed at them as if they were ancient artifacts, and in a way they were. He gave a nod of appreciation to Oliver and bent closer to study the sketches, both done in colored pencil.

"Tell me again," Black Horn said, his long, gray braids hanging down, framing his narrow face and the lines marking his seventy-plus years. "Why did you decide to do these sketches?"

Oliver cleared his throat. He was a tall man, a characteristic that got in the way of his desire to be unobtrusive. He liked to be on the edges, just on the outside looking in, thrilled by the color of things, or the movement, or the serenity of a sunset. So it was natural for him to pick up a camera and record those moments in time. But never in his thirty-eight years did he ever have such a story to tell.

"Well," he began, "it was after I shot a couple dozen photographs of these two dancers."

He pointed at the sketches, one of a Lakota man and the other of a Lakota woman in what appeared to be pre-reservation period clothing. "When I tried to download them from the photo card to the computer, they weren't there. All the photos I took of them were gone. Other photos were there, hundreds of them of dancers from Rosebud, Pine Ridge, Cheyenne River, but nothing of these two people. It's like there were—"

"Ghosts," said Black Horn. "Sometimes ghosts—spirits— appear in photographs, and sometimes they don't."

"So that's what they are, these two?"

Black Horn pulled a chair close and sat. "Yeah," he said. "They are. Where did you see them?"

"Everywhere," Red Lance replied. "They were at Rosebud, then Pine Ridge, then Lower Brule, Crow Creek, and then Cheyenne River. I saw him in Lower Brule. A friend of mine told me about him," he said, pointing to the sketch of the man. "He was impressed with his costume. He noticed the elk hooves he wore instead of brass bells."

"When did the woman show up?"

"At Lower Brule. After that they both appeared at the other pow-wows, but not together, I mean they didn't dance together, they were just at the same pow-wow. Strange, huh?"

Black Horn nodded. "Could be."

"What do you think? Are they really ghosts? And why did so many people see them?"

The old medicine man smiled. "They are ghosts, spirits," he said. "Just because some people are skeptical or don't believe in them doesn't mean they're not around. So, how many people saw them, do you think?"

"Just about everyone, I would guess, who watched the dancing at the pow-wows. Hundreds of people saw them. When I asked other people to describe them to me, they described what I saw. So we were all seeing the same two people, same two ghosts, I mean."

"Yeah, you're right."

Red Lance pointed at the sketches. "I photographed these," he said. "They showed up on my photo card."

"Yeah, the sketches are physical things."

"Yup, so I made prints and I'll make as many as I can afford to. I want to give them away. Sort of as a reminder, I guess."

The old man nodded. "You could make a lot of money selling prints," he said.

"Yeah, I suppose. Doesn't seem right, though."

The medicine man nodded again. "That was the right answer."

"I want you to have these sketches. They're the originals. But, you know, I'm wondering what it all means. Why did they appear and why did so many people see them, at all those pow-wows?"

Black Horn stood and walked over to the coffeepot on the counter and poured two cups, and brought them to the table. "I think I know why," he admitted. "But, ah, first, I want to hear from some of the people who saw them. Do you suppose you could get a few of them together, and bring them here to my house? I want to hear their stories first."

"Yeah, yeah, I think I can do that, sure. When do you want us to come?"

So it was, that on a warm, late autumn afternoon seven people—three women and four men, including Oliver Red Lance—arrived at the home of Johnson Black Horn, not far from Gray Grass Creek on the northwest edge of the reservation. Agnes Black Horn, Johnson's wife, served a delicious buffalo meat and vegetable soup, and cups of peppermint tea and coffee.

The medicine man took them to the shade of four large, old cottonwood trees north of his house. There they saw lawn chairs arranged in a circle. Just west of the cottonwoods was a sweat lodge, with a bit of smoke rising from the embers still smoldering in the firepit. A sweat ceremony had apparently happened sometime before they arrived.

After they took their seats, the medicine man burned gray sage and smudged them all, and told them what he wanted.

"Thank you for coming," he said. "Oliver and I asked you here because of the two dancers you saw this past summer, at the pow-wows. I would like each one of you to tell what you saw. Then I'll tell you what I think," he paused, "and what I know." He indicated the young man on his left. "We'll start with you and go down the line."

Cameron Old Wolf was barely twenty-two, a slender, pleasant-looking young man with long hair. He had been a grass dancer since he could remember. His father was a grass dancer, as his grandfather had been.

"Do you believe in ghosts?" the medicine man asked him.

Old Wolf shrugged. "Never gave it much thought," he said softly. "I heard stories. But after the pictures I took of that traditional dancer weren't saved in my camera, like what happened to Oliver, I guess I sort of do, now."

"Tell us what happened," prompted the old man.

"The first thing I noticed was the elk hooves. He wore them like everyone wears the brass bells, tied around his knees and ankles." Old Wolf began. "I seen pictures of that kind of stuff, but I never saw anyone wearing anything but brass bells. I guess I noticed him because he danced quiet. Elk hooves rattle a bit, but they're not loud like bells. Then I noticed his breechclout was real, it wasn't wool or any kind of cloth. It was tanned hide. And his moccasins were not beaded, they were decorated with quills."

Nodding slowly the medicine man gazed thoughtfully at the ground beyond his feet. "Anything else that stood out, or was unusual to you?"

"Ah, he wore a breast plate made of real bones."

"How could you tell?"

"The bones were kind of dull looking. Plastic bones, the kind you buy at the craft stores, are exactly alike, and they're shiny."

Black Horn nodded.

"Oh, and he was kind of buffed, you know, in really good shape for his age. I noticed that cause he didn't wear a shirt."

"How old did he seem to you?"

"Ah, I guess maybe forties, or thereabouts."

"What songs did he dance to? Did you happen to notice that?"

The young man thought for a moment. "Yeah, come to think of it. He danced to only the men's traditional songs and the sneak-ups."

Johnson Black Horn glanced up as the murmur of the cottonwood leaves grew with a sudden breeze. Most of the leaves were still green. He shot a quick look at the woman to the left of Old Wolf. She was tall and her face was strong and classically beautiful with obvious Lakota features.

"You don't dance so much anymore, do you?"

She nodded. "No, just now and then. It's more about my kids and grandkids now. My husband and I are the pow-wow chaperones, I guess."

"*Tunjan*, when did you first see the dancers?"

"Here," Blanche LaDeau said, "at Rosebud, at our pow-wow, and then at Pine Ridge."

Black Horn had called her "niece," rather than "granddaughter" in Lakota because she was older than Cameron Old Wolf, perhaps early forties.

"Both of them, or just one?"

"Both, I saw both of them. I saw the woman first. I noticed all the elk teeth sewn on the yoke of her dress, dozens of them. I was dancing behind her and I tried to get closer to get a better look. Funny thing was, I couldn't. Then when the song stopped, she just seemed to blend in with the other dancers and I couldn't see her anywhere."

"Did she have anything in her hands?"

"Yeah, an eagle wing fan, ah, in her left hand."

Black Horn looked off into the distant prairie, as if trying to visualize the image. "Anything else about her, anything she was wearing?"

"Yeah, eagle plumes tied to her braids."

The medicine man nodded slowly. "And her braids, were they hanging down her back or over her chest, in the front?"

LaDeau thought for a moment. "Ah, down the front. Oh, yeah, isn't that how married women wore their braids in the old days?"

"They did," Black Horn affirmed. "Women could show their standing by the streamers they tied to the ends of their braids."

"That's right," said the elderly woman four chairs down the line. She was small and thin, with dark, gentle eyes and wore two long, gray braids. Her name was Alice Yellow Hand. "A red streamer shows her husband was wounded in battle," she went on. "A black streamer shows her husband was killed in battle. An eagle plume was to show that she was a widow and never remarried after her husband was killed, or died serving the people. To be one of the 'Only Ones' brought honor to her family. She was a woman who had a high standing in the community. All women were respected and treated with courtesy. But an Only One was an example for all girls and young women to follow. She was respected and revered by all the men in the community and referred to as 'Auntie' or 'Mom' or 'Grandma' by them, whether they were related to her or not."

The older woman's words brought a respectful silence to the circle. All the men nodded.

"Thank you, *hankasi*." Black Horn said after a moment, addressing Alice Yellow Hand as "cousin." He cast an inclusive glance around. "Did you see any feathers on her head, up or hanging down?"

Most of the people shook their heads to indicate they hadn't.

"Why do you ask?" Blanche LaDeau wondered.

"Women didn't wear feathers on their head the same way men did a long time ago. The only exception was if they had fought in a battle."

After a momentary silence, LaDeau said, "So women today shouldn't be wearing feathers as part of our dance regalia?"

"No," replied the medicine man. "Except for women veterans."

"Yeah," Alice Yellow Hand added. "But it's hard to tell people anything these days. They get offended. I said that years ago to a woman I know. She told me to mind my own business. She still wears two feathers when she dances."

A slightly uncomfortable silence settled in for a moment. "But you know, not all men are entitled to wear a full feather bonnet," pointed out Black Horn. "Not even tribal presidents, just because they're a tribal president. At the very least, only elders should wear them."

After another moment, he turned to LaDeau. "What about the man dancer? What did you notice about him?"

LaDeau pointed at Cameron Old Wolf. "Like he said, I noticed his elk hoof bells first, then the quillwork on his leggings. The dye on the quills wasn't bright, you know, like modern paints and dyes are. They were like old photographs I've seen."

Most of the other people nodded in silent affirmation.

Blanche LaDeau glanced around and then briefly at the medicine man. "So that man, or whoever made his regalia, looked at old photographs and copied them?"

"Is that what you think?" Black Horn asked.

LaDeau shook her head. "I don't know what to think, really."

"Why is that?" asked Black Horn.

"Oh, I suppose because, probably like everyone here," the woman said, throwing up her hands, "I saw them only in the arena. I didn't see them walking around, or sitting and resting like most dancers do. Then when the intertribal songs were sung, there they were again, dancing. I didn't see either of them walk into the arena. They were just there."

The medicine man glanced around at the others. They were all nodding in agreement, but their faces wore a variety of expressions, from confusion to doubt. He turned to the woman next to LaDeau. She was another younger person, perhaps late twenties or early thirties.

"My name is Theresa Heard," she said. "I live over by the casino with my family. I'm a jingle dress dancer and my husband is a traditional dancer. Our kids dance, too."

"Which one did you see?" Black Horn asked her.

"Both, I saw them both, but the woman first."

"I see. Was it like *Tunjan* Blanche said, I mean as far as the quills and what she carried?"

Theresa Heard nodded. "Yeah. She described everything I noticed about her."

"Uh-huh. Let me ask you, did she look at anyone, did she make eye contact?"

Heard pondered for a moment. "No, she didn't. She kept her eyes down. I never noticed her looking up at anyone, or even looking around."

"Same for the man?"

The woman nodded emphatically. "Yeah, he didn't look at anyone. And something else I noticed, that no one's mentioned so far, is the lance he carried."

"A lance? What was it like?"

She laced her fingers together and looked up at the cottonwood leaves for a moment. "Well," she said, "I think it was made from a branch or a small tree."

"What do you mean?"

"The knots. I saw knots on the stick where the small branches were, and it wasn't smooth like a broomstick, or a dowel."

"You have sharp eyes," Black Horn complimented.

"I'm a mom and a teacher, I notice things. Oh, and something else. The point—well, actually there were two points. The top one was longer and wider than the one on the bottom end. It was smaller, no wider than the stick. And they looked like they were made from stone."

The man next to Theresa Heard raised a hand. His name was Lucas Iron Wing. Of all the men in the group, he was the only one with short hair. Black Horn remembered that he was a laboratory technician at the hospital.

"*Leksi*," he said to the medicine man. "I'm just as traditional as anyone here, but I'm not so sure these people we're talking about are ghosts, exactly. Maybe they just know how to make things the old way. You know? Maybe they're just trying to drum up business."

Black Horn nodded. "Yeah, okay. So did they hand out business cards, or did they have a vendor booth? Did you see them talking to anyone?"

"I don't know," Iron Wing admitted. "I see what you're getting at. Everyone who has anything to sell usually has a booth, or they show their stuff around."

"Did the man have a bustle?" Black Horn suddenly wondered.

Heads shook all around, and "No" was murmured here and there.

"And the woman, did she carry a shawl like some traditional woman dancers do?"

Same response.

Iron Wing leaned forward in his chair. "So, *Leksi*," he said, looking at the medicine man for a long moment. "Are you saying that the way they were dressed is unusual in some way?"

Black Horn sighed. "In the old days people would dance in their—well, let's say their good clothes. Everyday clothing was plain and undecorated. It was the clothing worn to important gatherings or social occasions that was decorated, for both men and women. I'm not sure when what we call 'dance regalia' came along, but when we dance today we put on all that regalia. So what you saw was two dancers wearing the ceremonial clothes of their time."

"That's why they stood out," suggested Iron Wing. "They were just different enough."

"I would say so," Black Horn agreed.

The young man pursed his lips and blew out a long breath. "*Leksi*, so are the man and woman we all saw, are they really ghosts?"

The medicine man smiled patiently. "What do you think?"

"I think they are ghosts," said Alice Yellow Hand. Except for the medicine man, she was the oldest person in the circle. "I know they are."

"What makes you so sure?" asked the young man, Cameron Old Wolf.

"A feeling, like when I felt someone sit on the edge of my bed, after my husband died. It was my husband, I know it."

Black Horn nodded at the woman. "So when did you first see them?"

"Here," Alice Yellow Hand replied. "And then again up at Cheyenne River. "I have relatives up there so I always go to that celebration. I seen them both, the woman first."

Black Horn gestured toward the first four people in the circle. "And it was the same as what they said?"

She nodded. "Yeah. Everything but the man's lance."

"Oh? He wasn't carrying anything when you saw him?"

"He was, he was, but it wasn't a lance. It was a long bow, curved backward at the handle, with a point at the bottom end.

I seen pictures of those kinds of bows. I think they're called medicine bows, or maybe society bows."

The medicine man nodded slowly before he looked up at the others sitting in the circle. "Anyone else see a bow instead of a lance?"

The man sitting next to Oliver Red Lance raised his hand. "I saw what Mrs. Yellow Hand is describing. And, yes, I think it was a society bow. Some of the leaders of warrior societies carried those bows."

Johnson Black Horn looked at the man. Dark brown hair and light brown eyes indicated *wasicu*, or white, blood, but his features were definitely Lakota. He appeared to be in his mid- to late fifties, perhaps even sixty.

"John Bonner?"

Bonner nodded. "Yeah, my dad was John, Sr., and my mom was Maude White Bear. I grew up north of Two Kettle."

"You saw the bow?"

"Sure did. First thing I noticed. I saw both of them at Lower Brule. Interesting, don't you think, that two of us out of seven saw something different? Everything else you're all describing is what I saw, too."

Lucas Iron Wing raised a hand. "I saw pictures of that kind of bow, too. But, like I said, I saw the man carrying a lance."

"I think the Kit Fox Warrior Society leader carried a bow like that, in the old days," pointed out Alice Yellow Hand. "My great-great-grandfather was one of those."

"Was his name Yellow Hand—*Nape Zi*?"

The woman shook her head. "No, that's my husband's family. My great-great-grandfather's name was *Wahukeza Wakan*, Holy Lance."

Everyone noticed the medicine man's sideways glance toward the sweat lodge as a curious expression briefly flashed across his face.

John Bonner spoke again. "*Leksi*," he said to Black Horn, using the word for "uncle" as a sign of respect. "You think there's some kind of connection to Mrs. Yellow Hand's great-great-grandfather, because of the society bow?"

Black Horn nodded slowly as he sat, apparently deep in thought, his eyes fixed on something in his own awareness. In a moment he pulled himself from whatever he was seeing and looked at the others.

"Yeah, I think so," he told them. "These kinds of things don't happen just by chance. The unusual thing here is that those two ghosts were seen by so many people in several different places."

"I think I see a pattern here," John Bonner pointed out. "The places we saw them is important, I think. I mean the pow-wows themselves."

Black Horn nodded, more in encouragement than agreement. "Yeah."

Bonner continued. "All the pow-wows where they were seen are old, in that they've been going on for a long time. This year Rosebud's pow-wow is going on one hundred forty years. And—and it started as a victory celebration for Little Bighorn. All the others are ongoing celebrations as well."

The people in the circle glanced at one another at that realization.

"You're right," Black Horn agreed. "They didn't show up at the newer pow-wows, or at the ones indoors."

"Or at night," Alice Yellow Hand observed. "I saw them only in the daytime, the afternoon pow-wows."

Old Wolf was puzzled. "I think you're right. But what would that mean?"

Black Horn looked around, his expression indicating he knew the reason, and was waiting for someone to reveal it.

Blanche LaDeau ventured a guess. "I think it's because of the lights at night. There was no electricity in their time."

Black Horn smiled knowingly, nodding. He clasped his hands and leaned forward. "When I was a younger man, I went to visit my brother and his family. They lived along Gray Grass Creek, too, down in a valley. He had made a new road into his place, just a pasture trail, because the other road kept washing out.

"Anyway, we were all sitting at their kitchen table. We had a view of the new road out the window. One of us noticed a man near the road, and we all saw him at a distance, and then he came close, about forty yards. He did a strange thing. He squatted and looked at the road. Then he stood, and jumped into the air. He floated above the road and came down in the grass on the other side."

The others in the circle were listening in rapt attention.

"Later I told my dad, he was still alive then. He said the man we saw was a ghost and though he was on land he knew, he didn't know the road. It was new to him, so he wouldn't use it because it didn't exist in his time."

No one in the circle, especially the older ones, was surprised by Black Horn's story. There were many such on any reservation. Traditional Lakota people knew that many beings shared this physical existence with them, even though some dwelt in another realm.

"My grandpa told me a story like that," Alice Yellow Hand said. "We lived by the river where there was a sharp bend. He used to see a woman in a buckskin dress carrying water bags to a spot in a meadow, and dip her bags as if getting water. But the stream was a few yards away. Grandpa said she did that because that's where the river used to be, a long time ago."

"Did our people have dances at night?" wondered Cameron Old Wolf.

"Oh, yeah," Black Horn replied. "They danced around a fire, it was at the center."

"I know they didn't call them 'pow-wows,'" the young man declared.

"No, they didn't," the medicine man concurred. "Dances, they called them—*wacipi*. There were social dances, and some ceremonial such as the Calling-the-Buffalo Dance, the Eagle Dance, and others. Whenever there was a feast or a community gathering, there was usually dancing. It was a way to acknowledge and celebrate life. Dancing was overall a good thing."

"And I'll bet there was no prize money," Blanche LaDeau said, chuckling.

Black Horn chuckled. "No, there sure wasn't. Our ancestors didn't need that kind of incentive to dance."

"Cousin," Alice Yellow Hand injected quietly, addressing the medicine man. "Why do *you* think we saw those two spirits? Why did *they* show themselves to so many people in different places?"

"Good question, and the right one," replied Black Horn. He took a deep breath, exhaled, and pointed toward the sweat lodge.

"Earlier today, my helpers and I did a sweat," he told everyone, "and we asked that question about the *wacihipi*, the man and woman who came to dance. And the answer is very simple, and at the same time it puts a responsibility in front of us, if we want it."

They all waited as the medicine man paused.

"They came to remind us who and what we are, and that there is strength in who and what we are. And—and to scold us for losing our way."

Everyone silently considered the medicine man's words, the words that came from the two ghosts through him. A silence, except for the murmuring cottonwood leaves, hung for several long moments as seven people pondered what they had just heard.

"I guess I don't understand, Grandpa," said Cameron Old Wolf. "I know our ancestors had a strong culture, but they couldn't defeat the white man."

"There are different ways to be strong," Alice Yellow Hand said.

"You're right, both of you," Black Horn replied. "Our ancestors didn't have enough warriors and enough guns to drive the white men out. That doesn't mean they lacked courage. They faced overwhelming odds and still fought. What we should think about is how we survive to this day when white people and their government and their churches tried—and are still trying—to take everything away from us."

"The old ways," said John Bonner. "We survived because enough of us remembered the old ways. We didn't survive because we assimilated, although some of us think so."

"That's true." Alice Yellow Hand asserted. "But we are not our ancestors. They were strong. We may think of ourselves as Lakota today, but we are not as strong as they were."

"What does that mean?" Old Wolf asked.

"What language are we speaking right now?" the medicine man asked cautiously.

"Well, English," Old Wolf hesitantly replied.

"And why?"

The young man shrugged, looking a bit puzzled. "It's what everyone does, right?"

"Yeah, but how did it come to be that way?" Black Horn persisted gently.

Alice Yellow Hand leaned forward in her chair. Her first glance was at Cameron Old Wolf, and then her gaze swept the others in the circle as well.

"Because our own language was taken from us. In my grandma and grandpa's time the government and Catholic boarding schools punished kids when they spoke it. When I went to the boarding school a nun locked me in a closet, all day, for speaking Lakota. It was dark and hard to breathe. I had to lie on the floor and get air from the space at the bottom of the door."

The others in the circle glanced at the older woman, their expressions ranging from shock to sympathy.

"So I was really careful after that," she said. "When I told my grandma, she cried, and then she told me to whisper it the next time."

Alice Yellow Hand reached up slowly to wipe away a tear sliding down her face. "*Eyas hecena Lakoleyewaye*," she said, and then translated her own words. "But I still speak Lakota."

"Thank you, cousin, for telling us," Black Horn said to the woman. He turned to the others. "There are lots of stories like hers, too many. It's a miracle we still have our language. It's a miracle because of people like Alice."

Cameron Old Wolf raised his hand. "So, ah, what does being punished for speaking Lakota have to do with the dancers, you know, the ghosts?"

Johnson Black Horn smiled patiently. "Everything," he said gently. "And a lot more."

"I sure would like to know what that is," John Bonner said.

Black Horn glanced around at each of the faces in the circle, a penetrating, assessing gaze. He sighed and sat straighter in his chair.

"Those ghosts came for a reason," he began. "They came to let us know that too many of us have forgotten who we are. For too many of us, the only part of us that's Lakota is our skin. They came to remind us that we have to be Lakota in the way we think, the way we live, and in the way we treat each other. Too many of us have forgotten where we came from; we've forgotten our ancestors, and we don't speak our language."

Blanche LaDeau nodded in agreement. "That is the truth," she said. "My dad used to say that if each one of us was as tall as how much we are Lakota," she gestured toward the medicine man, "in all those ways that you said, some of us would only be one foot tall."

The young man, Cameron Old Wolf, shuffled his feet nervously. "That's kind of harsh, you know? I don't think it's my fault that my folks didn't speak Lakota. So because of that, I didn't learn it."

"That's true," Black Horn agreed. "Still, you learned how to dance. You learned the songs. So maybe you could learn to speak Lakota. Our university teaches it, or I think someone would be willing to teach you. It's up to you."

The young man shrugged. "I work a full-time job. It'll be hard to find the time," he countered.

No one spoke for several seconds.

John Bonner cleared his throat. "I read a report done by some language institute, I think it was," he said carefully. "One of the statistics showed there were only about twenty-four hundred first language Lakota speakers left on our rez. And I don't think any one of those people are younger than sixty-five or so. And I believe our population is about thirty-eight thousand. So that means, if my math is right, less than ten percent of us are first language speakers. Not too long ago there were six thousand Lakota speakers."

Blanche LaDeau was shocked. "Is that true?"

"I sure as hell hope not," Lucas Iron Wing blurted. "Because that sounds like we're losing our language when all those people are gone."

Black Horn nodded somberly. "It's true," he said sadly.

"My goodness," LaDeau was shocked, "that's so scary. So when all those first language speakers are gone, what's going to happen then?"

Bonner threw up his hands. "I think there's a good chance we lose connection to the old form of the language," he pointed out. "Our first language speakers learned it from other first language speakers, like their parents and grandparents. That way there was a connection to the usage of the past, you know, the

way our great- and great-great-grandparents spoke it. Languages
change over time. But if we're left with people, Lakota people,
who learned to speak Lakota as a second language, their fluency
may not be as good as a first language speaker. So we lose that
connection to the old form."

Lucas Iron Wing gazed intently at Bonner. "Don't take this
the wrong way," he said. "But how do you know all that?"

Bonner smiled. "I know I look like a *wasicu* but I'm a first
language speaker. My mom's parents, my grandparents, lived
with us when I was growing up, and the three of them spoke
Lakota all the time. That's how I learned it."

"Okay," the younger man said, "but isn't it better to have a
lot of second language speakers than no Lakota language at all?"

"Of course," Bonner allowed. "But I think we have to stick
to the old form as much as possible. Look, here's an example
of what's happening. I hear a lot of people say *Hinhanni Waste*,
which is a translation of 'good morning.' But that greeting was
never used in the old days. So when people say that in Lakota
now, it's not correct. And some of us first language speakers feel
we're changing our language to cater to the colonizers."

"Colonizers?" Iron Wing was puzzled. "You mean white
folks?"

"Yeah."

"Okay, I get it. So how should we greet each other?"

Black Horn softly cleared his throat. "We do that by saying our relationship to the person we're talking to." He nodded
toward Blanche LaDeau. "Like I said to her, I called her *Tunjan*,
or 'niece.' Then I would say something appropriate, like *Tanyan
wacinyankelo,* which is, 'It's good to see you.' Or I might say,
Tanyan yahi yelo, which is, 'It's good that you came.' We didn't
use anything like 'good morning' or 'good night.'"

A low chuckle came from the youngest member of the
group, Cameron Old Wolf. "That's kind of like splitting hairs,

isn't it? I mean, as long as someone is speaking the language, why should it matter?"

Alice Yellow Hand shook her head, a hint of exasperation in her eyes. "Because we're changing it to please the whites," she snapped. "A priest asked my grandpa how we say 'god' in Lakota. My grandpa told him we don't have a word that means what 'god' means in their way. He said we use *Wakan Tanka* and that means something bigger and more powerful and more sacred than we can describe. The priest kind of laughed, like he didn't believe that. And then he said, 'What does it really mean?' They do that to our language, if they can't understand something, they change it or they make fun of it.

"And one more thing," Alice Yellow Hand added. "I don't like drum groups singing round dance songs in English. I really don't like that. Those are our songs, not theirs."

Johnson Black Horn nodded, a twinkle in his eye. The young man, Old Wolf, stared at the ground.

After a moment of utter silence, John Bonner raised a hand. "*Leksi*," he said to Black Horn. "You said you did an *Inipi*, a sweat. Was it about the dancers we saw?"

Black Horn looked up and nodded slowly. "It was."

"Is it something you can tell us?" Bonner ventured hopefully.

"Yeah, I can," replied the medicine man.

The circle of faces gazed at him, expressions ranging from anticipation to uncertainty.

"The Spirits told us that the dancers brought a simple message, and it is for us Lakota today to regain our past ways and beliefs and use them to save ourselves."

After several moments of silence, John Bonner looked around at the other people. "That's a powerful message," he said. "I'm guessing they didn't provide explicit instructions for us to follow."

Black Horn smiled and shook his head. "No, they didn't. It's up to us figure it out and do it. But, you know, it is plain enough to me."

"Well, we have a lot of problems, that's for sure," Alice Yellow Hand declared. "Drugs, alcohol—especially that meth—broken families, diabetes, suicides, no jobs. Seems like it gets worse every year."

"How is the past going to save us from all that stuff?" Old Wolf asked. "What does the past have to do with what's happening today?"

Alice Yellow Hand shot an annoyed glance at the young man and looked away quickly, but said nothing. In another moment she glanced at the medicine man. "My grandpa used to say we should have listened to Sitting Bull, you know, the vision he had before the Greasy Grass Fight."

Everyone but John Bonner seemed confused.

"What do you mean?" asked Lucas Iron Wing. "I thought that was a vision about a victory over the soldiers."

"It was," Black Horn affirmed. "But there was more to it. Most of us know about it. Sitting Bull was given a vision at his Sun Dance, about a month before the Greasy Grass. Soldiers and their horses were falling from the sky into a Lakota village. A voice said, 'I give you these because they have no ears.' But the last part of what the voice said was, 'Take nothing that belongs to them.'"

Iron Wing persisted. "What does it mean, that last part?"

"I think it has two meanings," Black Horn told him. "Don't take anything that belongs to them means what they have in their hands, and then their ways."

"During the fighting," John Bonner said, "and afterward, our fighting men took rifles and pistols and ammunition. I understand why they did. Not all of the warriors had firearms and it was a battle. So it was sort of natural to pick up a rifle and shells. After the battle, though, some of the people stripped the dead soldiers, and took personal effects. I always thought they shouldn't have done any of that, because of the vision."

"Me, too," Black Horn agreed. "But there's something else. Afterward, when the missionaries came and they took our children and put them in boarding schools, they began to teach them their ways, their language. Those are things of theirs, if we want to look at it that way."

Lucas Iron Wing was puzzled. "I guess I don't understand what you mean," he admitted. "Our ancestors had no choice. The buffalo were all gone, right? So they had to use canvas to make tipis, and after a while they starting living in log houses, ah, square houses. And they started wearing white man's clothing. What choice did they have?"

"Really good point, Lucas," Bonner agreed. "I've often wondered if Sitting Bull's vision wasn't referring to the soldiers' guns. Maybe 'take nothing of theirs' meant the ways of the white people, their beliefs, traditions, customs, and language. How many of us today truly think and act and function with the same values and norms our Lakota ancestors lived by? Look at how some of us disregard and disrespect our elders, and how we treat our women. And there was a time when leadership was a responsibility, not a prize or a source of privilege or power. I mean, we govern ourselves the way the whites told us to, right?"

"The less Lakota we are the more problems we have," Alice Yellow Hand observed. "Some of us remember the old ways, I know that. But most of us who call ourselves Lakota don't follow them. Just because we wear white people's clothes and live in square houses and drive cars, does that mean we have to act like they do, and believe what they do?"

Blanche LaDeau leaned forward and gazed at the old woman. "I think I know what you mean. We can still be Lakota on the inside, right? Where it counts?"

The old woman smiled. "White people's clothes on the outside doesn't mean we have to have white people's ways and thoughts on the inside."

"Let me tell you something that happened to me last year, with the kids in my class," Theresa Heard offered. "It was during a history lesson. My class knew who the president of the United States was, and some of the past presidents. They knew some other white historical figures, like Abraham Lincoln and George Washington. But when I asked them who Sitting Bull was, only a few knew. Most of them heard about Crazy Horse, and Spotted Tail. But when I asked them who our tribal president is now, none of them knew."

"So what does that mean?" Cameron Old Wolf blurted.

"It means, I think, that we know more about white history and culture than we do about our own," Heard retorted.

After an uncomfortable, deep silence, John Bonner spoke. "Little Lakota boys can tell you what an Xbox One or PlayStation is, but not all of them know what an Iktomi, you know, the Trickster story is," he pointed out sadly. "Our kids know more about Star Wars culture than Lakota culture. Their heroes are rappers, Captain America, Iron Man, and Thor. They mimic the in-your-face, take-no-crap style of Han Solo, but they know nothing of a true hero like Crazy Horse. They'll pester their parents for the money to go see a Star Wars or a Transformers movie, but they won't sit and listen to their grandma or grandpa tell stories, for free."

"That's pretty tough criticism of our kids," Blanche LaDeau stated. "I think you're right though, you know. I wonder where that disconnect started—in what generation, I mean."

"With the schools and churches," Alice Yellow Hand declared. "With bible stories and *wasicu* fairy tales. 'Jack and the Beanstalk' and 'Ring Around the Rosie' took the place of our own stories."

Lucas Iron Wing cleared his throat, a bit uncomfortably. "So, I guess that means we're living more of a white lifestyle than a Lakota one."

"There's another side to that which most of us don't see," John Bonner asserted. "All the movies that our kids and grand-kids like—and they like them so much they buy all the action figures—they all have a hidden message. It's really subtle. Maybe that's the way to describe it. Subtle racism. All the heroes, or most of them, are muscle-bound white males that are practically indestructible and always overcome incredible odds."

Theresa Heard agreed. "Yeah, I always thought that, too. They send a message to our Native kids, our brown-skinned kids—that you can't be a hero, or good, or smart, unless you're white."

"So the mythical heroes our kids grow up emulating are not good role models for them?" Lucas Iron Wing asked.

"They're the wrong ones," Bonner persisted. "Society, or maybe more to the point, capitalism, is shoving the wrong things down their throats. So it's darn hard for the quiet grandma and grandpa voices that tell stories of real heroes, like Crazy Horse and Sitting Bull and Buffalo Calf Road. It's darn hard to com-pete with the loud, multimillion-dollar movies with all their fake heroes."

"Ah, who's Buffalo Calf Road?" Cameron Old Wolf asked. "What's his tribe?"

Bonner smiled patiently. "*She* was Northern Cheyenne. She fought in a battle with her brother, saved his life as a matter of fact. She rescued him after his horse was shot, rode through an enemy crossfire to do it. Whites call it the Rosebud Battle, eight days before Little Bighorn. Lakota and Cheyenne call it The Battle Where the Girl Saved Her Brother."

"Oh," Old Wolf replied, almost inaudibly. "Nobody told me those stories," he admitted. "I mean, I've heard a few, but

I sure would like to hear more. That Buffalo Calf Road, she sounds like a badass."

Alice Yellow Hand looked at him with a piercing, angry gaze. "Like a what?"

"Oh, no, no, it's nothing derogatory," he assured her quickly. "It means she's as tough and brave as they come."

"Oh," she relented. "So that's what it means."

As a few soft chuckles floated through the air, John Bonner cleared his throat and leaned forward. "Uncle," he said to the medicine man, "so the dancers we all saw, they came to tell us to remember who we are?"

Black Horn nodded slowly. "In a way. They told us to use our old ways and beliefs to save ourselves. That means the answers to the problems are there in the past, with everything that made us a strong people. Makes sense to me. Two things come to my mind—diabetes and all the young people committing suicide. Our people have diabetes because we don't eat what our ancestors did, like buffalo, elk, and deer meat, and all the berries and the *tinpsila*, what they call "wild turnip." If we go back to that and stay away from sugar and lard and potato chips and pop and meat wrapped in plastic we can have our health back."

"What about the suicides?" Lucas Iron Wing asked.

"I think it's because a lot of young people really don't know who they are," replied the medicine man. "Knowing who you are is identity, it's—it's strength. It's like a shield we all need to defend ourselves when something attacks us, like racism, and doubt, or confusion—just about anything. They don't know enough about Lakota ways to have that shield. They don't know our history, their own family's history, they don't know where they came from."

"I agree with that," Alice Yellow Hand declared forcefully. "We did not give that shield to our children and grandchildren, because they grew up knowing the white man's ways. Every generation became weaker."

"Well," John Bonner said, "the government and the churches made it really hard, we can't forget that. And even now they certainly aren't doing anything to help. Schools don't teach our history. Racism is still a fact of life for us. Look what happened to those kids in Rapid City. White people pour beer on them, hurl insults, and the court let them get away with it."

"Yeah," Alice Yellow Hand agreed. Then said, sadly, "But still we should have tried harder. Now our grandchildren are suffering."

"The dancers came to remind us who we are," Johnson Black Horn asserted. "To remind us we still have the chance to go back to the old ways. If we do, we have a chance to teach our young ones, so they can grow up strong and know who they are."

"So, the dancers, were they anyone in particular?" Theresa Heard asked. "Or just representations of the past?"

The medicine man looked around at the circle of faces. He had no idea if they would believe what he was about to tell them, or how it would affect them. But he had been given a task, a very important task, and he would do as he was asked.

"Some of the spirits that come to us in our ceremonies," he began, "have lived on this Earth before. Some have not and are very, very old. It was the Old Ones who sent the two dancers.

"The woman's people lived to the north, along the river. Her name was *Pejuta To Win*, Blue Medicine Woman. In her life she was a good, strong woman who rode into battle with her husband a few times. She knew about a special medicine for women, from a thistle plant. She lived to be an old, old grandmother and told stories to all the children in the village."

The medicine man paused and allowed the others to absorb and contemplate the information he gave them. Then he looked toward Alice Yellow Hand and caught her gaze. "The man's name was *Wahukeza Wakan*, Holy Lance. Your great-great-grandfather," he told her. "Maybe you can tell us what you know about him."

The old woman was surprised at the medicine man's revelation, and moved by the realization that she had seen her own great-great-grandfather. She nodded slowly and took a small handkerchief from her sleeve and dabbed at the tears in her eyes.

"My grandpa told me stories of his grandfather," she began. "Holy Lance was a good man, he said. He provided for his family and for anyone who needed his help. He was one of the headmen of the *Tokalas,* the Kit Fox Society. He was wounded in a fight with Crows, rescuing another warrior. He died a few days after that. He didn't live to be an old man."

Johnson Black Horn noted the various reactions to Alice's words, ranging from surprise to respect. The only skeptic seemed to be the youngest of the group, Cameron Old Wolf.

"Uncle," Blanche LaDeau spoke up softly, "since they came back to remind us that the answers are found in the past, where do we start? How do we go about it?"

The medicine man nodded thoughtfully. "Well," he began, "my nephew Oliver came to show me something a couple of weeks ago, and he told me about the dancers. So, I asked him to invite some people who had also seen them to come here, and here you are. I don't think it was by accident that each one of you is here, especially since one of you is actually related to one of the dancers. Each one of you can do something to answer that question of yours—'How do we go about it?' We need to think, and pray, and find the way."

"Will you do a ceremony?" John Bonner asked.

Black Horn nodded. "Yes, tonight, in my ceremony house. You're all welcome to be there."

"And then I think we should have an old time *wacipi*," suggested Alice Yellow Hand. "We should do it at night, around a fire, the way they did in the old days." She smiled. "Maybe the dancers we saw will come and join us."

"We will do that," the medicine man promised. He pointed toward Gray Grass Creek. "In the meadow, over there. Put out the word, all of you. We will have a feast and an old time dance, traditional songs and dances only."

Black Horn glanced at Oliver Red Lance. "My nephew has been very quiet," he told the others. "But he's the main reason you're here today. He has a gift for you."

The artist grabbed the large, flat, black portfolio next to his chair and stood up. "I'm glad that you came," he began. "I invited a lot of people, but you're the ones who showed up. About a week ago I came to visit Uncle, to ask him about some photographs I took, or tried to take, at the pow-wows over this past summer. You all know what happened, and I think the same happened to some of you. The pictures I took of the two dancers we're talking about didn't show up in my camera. All the other pictures of the pow-wows did. So, since I'm an artist, I sketched a picture of each of the dancers I saw."

Red Lance opened the portfolio and pulled out the color prints he had made from the originals. "I want each of you to have these," he said.

He stepped in front of each person and gave them two prints, one of the man and the other of the woman.

"Thank you," John Bonner exclaimed. "You're a very good artist."

Alice Yellow Hand was especially appreciative. "Now I can see my great-great-grandfather anytime I want." She reached out to shake the young man's hand. "Thank you."

And so it was that two weeks later, just over a hundred men, women, and children arrived for a feast and a *wacipi* in Johnson Black Horn's meadow. They had been instructed to park their cars near his house, and walk down to the area marked out in a dancing circle. Among them were Oliver Red Lance, Cameron Old Wolf, Blanche LaDeau, Alice Yellow Hand, Theresa Heard, Lucas Iron Wing, and John Bonner. Old Wolf, LaDeau, and Heard were dressed and prepared to dance.

Black Horn and John Bonner had talked the tribal president into donating a buffalo for the feast. Dozens of women worked to prepare the meal. The menu was simple and ancient: buffalo soup with wild turnips and onions, and gallons of wild peppermint tea. Dessert was *wojapi*, which is "boiled and thickened," and it was a sweet concoction made from chokecherries, sometimes called "fruit soup."

The meal was served in the old way as well, with young women taking the kettles of soup and pots of tea to the people as they sat in a circle around the marked-out dancing arena. The servers ladled the soup into each person's bowl and poured tea into individual cups.

While the people ate, a strong-voiced man, selected by Johnson Black Horn for this special duty, stood and spoke to the people. He was the *Eyapaha*, the "one who announces." He told the people that four drum groups had been invited to sing the songs. They had been invited because they knew the old songs and because the dancing would be traditional only.

Just before sundown, the wood in the center firepit would be lit, and when the flames were high the dancing would begin. Cameras or cell phones would be allowed, even encouraged, because Johnson Black wanted photographs and recordings of an old-time *wacipi* to be widely distributed.

There would be no prize money, just singing and dancing as the ancestors did, for the pure enjoyment and love of it.

At sundown, Johnson Black Horn and another medicine man helped an old man and an old woman start the fire. When the fire was high a signal was given, and the first drum group struck the first beat and lifted their voices into song.

No one counted the number of dancers, but estimates were given later. Some said as many as sixty, with a roughly equal split between men and boys and women and girls.

The moon rose just after dusk, casting an ethereal glow over the meadow. Adding to the otherworldliness of the evening, the flames from the fire danced to the drums as well, casting the dancers' shadows against the circle of night.

Drumbeats pounded strongly, and song after song rose into the pale light of the moonlit sky, echoing the very rhythm of the heartbeat of Grandmother Earth. It was a night and a moment in their lives that all who danced and sang and watched would not soon forget. It was a night when they connected with something very old, and very strong.

Some would mention later that they did not recognize two of the dancers, a man and a woman. They did not wear the usual regalia, they would say. The woman wore a buckskin dress decorated with quills and rows of elk teeth, an eagle wing fan in her hand, with eagle plumes tied to long braids that hung well below her waist. And the man did not wear a bustle on his back or a deer hair roach on his head, but he did carry a long, curved bow with a lance point. Several people noticed that he did not wear brass bells. Instead, tied around his ankles and knees were elk hooves. A very unusual thing for dancers to wear, they said, in this day and age.

And no one could remember where the two unknown dancers had gone after the dancing was over. No one had seen them leave. But Johnson Black Horn knew who they were, and so did Oliver Red Lance, and six other people who had prints of the colored pencil sketches of them hanging on their walls.

They also knew something the other people at Johnson Black Horn's old-time *wacipi* did not know. They knew why the two unknown dancers had come.

Red Lance had not given a title to the sketches of the dancers, so Alice Yellow Hand and the others simply called them *Wacihipi Hena*—The Ones Who Came to Dance.

About the Author

Joseph M. Marshall III was born and raised on the Rosebud Sioux Reservation and holds a PhD from Sinte Gleska University, which he helped to establish. The award-winning author of ten books, including *Hundred in the Hand*, *The Lakota Way*, and *The Long Knives Are Crying*, he has also contributed to various publications and written several screenplays. Marshall's work as a cultural and historical consultant can be seen and heard in the Turner Network Television and DreamWorks epic television miniseries *Into the West*.